Guide to STAMP COLLECTING

Jiří Nováček

CHARTWELL
BOOKS, INC.

For copyright reasons this edition is
for sale only within the U.S.A.

This edition published in 1989 by
Chartwell Books, Inc.
A division of Book Sales, Inc.
110 Enterprise Avenue
Secaucus, New Jersey 07094

Prepared by
The Hamlyn Publishing Group Limited,
a division of The Octupus Publishing Group,
Michelin House, 81 Fulham Road, London SW3 6RB

Translated by Šimon Pellar
Stamp drawings by Ivan Kafka
Graphic design by Jaroslav Příbramský

Copyright © Artia, Prague 1984, 1989
ISBN 1-55521-392-8

Printed in Czechoslovakia by Tisk, Brno
2/10/08/51-02

CONTENTS

WHAT IS PHILATELY?

Is philately an art, a science or merely a hobby? We can pose these questions and many similar ones and still not get a comprehensive answer. Philately is just... philately. It is a unique phenomenon, which defies comparison and any definition will always need qualification.

It is interesting to note that, despite the enthusiasm which many women have shown for philately, it is mainly a masculine affair, a lifelong passion for men and boys of all ages, regardless of nationality or background. Anybody who takes time off from the cares of everyday life and sits down in peace and quiet to study his stamps will never be sorry for having taken up philately as a hobby, since the moments spent with his collection will be extremely rewarding.

RAVENNA

Line cancellation of a post office

In practical terms, philately is primarily nothing but the collecting and sorting of postage stamps, letters and other postal material. Whereas some philatelists never get beyond this stage, others will try to use their material to document a particular period, present a picture of a country, trace a major historical event or show colourful, detailed portraits of plants or animals. Some philatelists may decide to use their stamp collection to document major geographic discoveries or military campaigns or simply turn their stamps into an attractive herbarium or a miniature home art gallery. The possibilities are infinite. Every collection is different, expressing the individual taste of its creator, and one of the aims of this book is to tell you how to build a collection.

First, however, we should perhaps try to find out how old philately is. The exact date is, of course, impossible to discover. All we can be certain of is that stamp collecting began later than the postage stamp itself. It is also certain that the modest beginnings of philately are definitely a thing of the past.

It is, perhaps, the collector's good fortune that the early days of philately will never return. Can you imagine coming upon a piece of plaster or perhaps a lampshade pasted all over with the first, rare issues of various countries, stamps that you have been dying to own as long as you have been a collector, knowing only too well that you will never be able to have them? It is a regrettable fact that the early collectors simply pasted their stamps on walls as they would wallpaper and used them to decorate various objects, including furniture. Stamps that according to present catalogues would fetch four- or five-figure sums were originally appreciated only for their colour design.

For instance, advertisements common in London newspapers of the 1850s that sought "...a larger amount of postage stamps for papering a bedroom; orange and olive colour preferred", or stated "...will sell a trinket box decorated with 1600 postage stamps", were meant quite seriously. It makes one dizzy just to realize what priceless beauties these stamps must have been.

A somewhat more sophisticated approach to stamp collecting was shown by the people who purchased the first stamp album and the first stamp catalogue, both of which were printed in England in 1852. However, the modern collector would be dismayed by the rough and ready methods of those early days: stamps were commonly torn off letters and pasted into albums with bone glue. A tear here or a missing perforation there were not regarded too seriously.

However, the widespread use of postage stamps soon made philately a hobby that anyone could take up. If the budding philatelist himself received no mail he could ask his friends to save stamps from their letters for him and those that he lacked could be acquired in exchange for duplicates of those he already possessed. To collect stamps cost virtually nothing but there were already collections into which the owner had put not only a lot of creative energy but also money.

One of the world's largest and oldest stamp collections is that of the British royal family. For more than a century they have been adding single issues as well as whole sets to their vast collection, which today consists of more than 400 large albums with approximately 20,000 album sheets. The management of this priceless collection is now taken care of by a group of experts. However, the extraordinary character and value of the royal stamp collection need not discourage the novice. Indeed, with diligence, perseverance, and some general knowledge a fine collection may be built up from scratch and practically without any cost.

Most beginners will be probably interested to learn about the origin of the word philately. It is derived from two Greek words: *philos* meaning 'loving', and *ateleia* — 'free of tax or payment'. Mail bearing a stamp of the appropriate denomination is carried free and no extra payment is required on delivery.

The word philately was coined in France in the 19th century and originally signified an interest in labels representing the payment for postal services. In due course it also came to mean the systematic collection and study of postage stamps, postmarks, postcards and similar material.

The First Choice for a Collector

Philately is not concerned solely with postage stamps and a knowledgeable philatelist will also be enthusiastic about a letter carried by post but with no stamp affixed. Perhaps it is time to clarify who issues stamps today and who did so in the

A symbolic group sculpture in front of the UPU Building in Berne, Switzerland, representing people from the five continents relaying letters. The sculpture has become the official emblem of the UPU and has appeared on many stamps

past. The answer may seem obvious. Naturally, it is the post office, an organization that, in return for payment, carries and delivers mail of various kinds.

11

With only a few exceptions, every country in the world has its own state-run postal organization. These institutions are members of the Universal Postal Union (UPU). On the basis of mutual agreements all UPU members render services to all other members. In practice this means that a letter posted, say, in Frankfurt, West Germany, and addressed to a person living in São Paulo, Brazil, is guaranteed delivery by the Brazilian post although it bears German and not Brazilian stamps. It goes without saying that the German postal authorities will render the same service at any time to their Brazilian counterparts.

However, the history of postal services reveals that in the past things could be very different. Various independent German principalities, the Hanseatic towns, Belgium, Austria, Bohemia, Spain, Italy and other areas were at one time served by a postal system run by the princely house of Thurn-Taxis. One might well ask which country could lay claim to this multinational service, whose headquarters were for long located in Brussels and which many German states banned from crossing their territory.

It is also well known that in Imperial Russia there were, besides the state post, also posts run by the provincial governments — *zemstva*. The two postal systems existed side by side without competing for each other's business and, in fact, some of the provincial posts serviced territories larger than those of many a European kingdom. This is why philatelists prefer to use the term 'stamp country' or 'stamp territory'. Thus the Thurn-Taxis postal system represents an interesting and, indeed, very important stamp territory although the Thurn-Taxis family never held a single city. Just as philatelists still collect issues of the former Kingdom of Bavaria, although the independent Bavarian state has long ceased to exist, or of the defunct Papal States, there are more stamp-issuing territories than states found on the map today. It is up to the collector to decide what to collect. The times are long gone when people such as the famous Baron Ferrari used to collect stamps of the entire world. Modern philatelists must specialize in a stamp territory, whether it be a historical or a modern one.

The situation is further complicated by the fact that in a number of countries there were, apart from the state-run post, also private services operated by various business companies. At the end of the 19th century nearly all large German cities had private local posts delivering letters, parcels, money, etc. In Berlin alone there were several private postal companies and they were not small ones. These local companies issued many stamps, postcards and covers and advertised heavily to compete with rivals for a share of the business.

Private posts also existed elsewhere and their proprietors were not always necessarily citizens of the country in which their organization operated. For example, there was a German traders' post in Morocco and Russian tea traders ran a postal route in China. In fact private posts are an important part of philately. Before discussing them in detail, however, it is worth nothing that the printing of stamps and postal stationery remained in private hands and could not, therefore, be controlled.

Private postal organizations exist even today. In 1968 a company called Independent Postal Services of America was incorporated in the United States, employing some 20,000 people. As American law forbids private businesses to carry letters, the company specializes in the delivery of magazines, newspapers, printed matter and parcels. Under the heading printed matter also come greeting cards and, since these pre-printed messages that need only to be signed are sent by Americans in large numbers every year, the volume of business that the company gets is enormous. Well-known also is the case of the numerous private postal services that sprang up in Britain during the prolonged strike by British post office workers. These services did a lot of business, not only carrying mail across the Channel but also by issuing stamps aimed at the collector market.

Such private postal services constitute separate stamp-issuing territories. Their existence and the stamps they issue faithfully reflect the particular period and its political and economic conditions. Philatelists may incorporate material of this kind in collections of stamps of the country within which such posts operate. Alternatively, they may collect them separately or according to means of conveyance: for example, many traders' posts operated only on sea, coastal or inter-island routes. Another possibility is to disregard these stamps altogether since they are not the official issues of the country in question. In brief, every beginner must think very carefully about what direction he will take in building his collection, searching for new acquisitions and selecting his exhibits.

The Second Choice for a Collector

The amateur philatelist now knows that he must learn to

concentrate his efforts. He may decide to collect issues of old Saxony, for example, or postal documents of the Balkan Peninsula. In the latter case, he may want to limit his collection to a certain period, say, from the end of the Second World War to the present. Or he may prefer to collect the issues of newly independent African states over the past decade.

However, there is another, quite different approach to starting a stamp collection, in which it is not necessary to limit oneself to any single country or region, or even a particular period. In this kind of collection, called topical or thematic, the philatelist exhibits stamps with a certain subject or topic, be it chess, horse breeding, butterflies, advances in medicine — in short anything, because there are a thousand and one possible topics to choose from. The aim of such a collection is to document and illustrate the selected topic by philatelic means, i.e. by stamps from all over the world, postmarks and other relevant material. Of course, the owner of a topical collection must not only be fond of his chosen object but must also be thoroughly knowledgeable about it. His work does not merely involve the collecting and acquiring of stamps with the required pictures: he must also study the literature on the subject in detail. For example, if he decides to build his collection around the development of currency, he may also use stamps showing cities where important mints existed, or stamps bearing portraits of sovereigns or rulers who had certain coinages minted. However, study is also a must for someone who collects the stamps of a particular country. It is completely impossible to create a picture of the present or past life of a country without a thorough knowledge of its geography and history.

It would be a mistake to believe that collecting on a particular theme is concerned only with stamps and is therefore more varied or colourful and perhaps easier than other kinds of collecting. Even this approach requires some historical research. A collection dealing with man's exploration of space will be much more valuable if, in addition to those colourful stamps showing rocket lift-offs, it can also include, for example, a letter written by a scientist who speculated about rocketry long before the launching of the first artificial satellite.

It is only when a collector departs from the pre-printed album and ventures to build his collection along his own lines that he becomes a true philatelist.

The Third and Final Choice for a Collector

So much has been already said about what must be done before starting a collection that the beginner will perhaps feel that all the important decisions have now been taken. Nevertheless, there remains one other, which, though it may seem a minor point, is, however, very important for the appearance of the future collection. The beginner must decide beforehand whether to collect cancelled (used) or unused stamps.

A brief glance in the window of any philatelic agency or shop will reveal that unused stamps are not only more attractive but also more expensive than cancelled ones. Does it mean that a collection made up from unused stamps is more valuable? Actually there is no simple answer to this question. While unused stamps of a new issue are usually more expensive and are sold for at least their nominal value or its official equivalent in another currency, cancelled stamps can be had at a fraction of their face value. However, the rates for older issues may be quite different. For instance, German stamps from the 1923 inflation period that bear proof of having been used fetch very good prices on the market, while unused stamps of the same period are sold almost by weight. This is not a universal rule, however, because prices for unused and cancelled stamps are subject to fluctuation and may (or may not) change over the years. And so the question remains: what sort of stamps to choose and why.

The answer does not depend on current prices. A philatelist specializing in countries will usually give preference to used stamps because cancellations and other postmarks and defacements will enable him to study the various carriers used and, in some cases, even different uses for the same stamp issue. For instance, many administrative bodies are known to have used their postage stamps as postage due, official or telegraph stamps. Of course, such a use cannot be proved when a stamp is in mint condition. Cancelled stamps on the other hand can be employed to document the first and last day of use or validity as well as a possible use after the stamp was invalidated, or use within a restricted area and many other bits of information of interest to the philatelist. Another reason why many philatelists prefer used stamps stems from their conviction that a stamp constitutes a postal document only if used in a postal service.

Unused stamps, or rather the pictures forming their design,

are often a vivid testimony to the events of a particular period or the emotions associated with them. Topic collectors prefer unused specimens because their collections are not designed to document the carrier, validity, or use. What they are mainly interested in is the legibility of the stamp design because this is the reason for including the stamp in the collection. A cancellation will often hide an essential detail.

Again, there are exceptions to the rule. Sometimes even collectors specializing in countries intentionally include an unused stamp in their collection to show a printing error, a retouch and similar minute details that would be probably indiscernible under a postmark. On the other hand, topic collectors occasionally include a cancelled stamp in their collection if the cancellation is related to their topic in some way. It may be a special cancellation, or a postmark from the local post office at the place of birth or residence of an important person who features in the history of their topic, etc. In any case, such cancelled stamps should not be included in the regular set but should be inserted separately. The reasons for their inclusion should be given, together with a note of any interesting details.

It must be perfectly clear from the entire collection, especially that of modern (i.e. post-1870) issues, whether the collector specializes in cancelled or unused stamps and any exceptions must be justified. A collection composed of an arbitrary hotch-potch of used and unused stamps has a poor aesthetic quality and, if exhibited, would be awarded a lower score by the jury.

All this should be made clear to the novice philatelist before he even starts collecting his material. The following chapters will deal with various kinds of philatelic material — and not only postage stamps — used to build a collection.

STAMPS AND THEIR ORIGIN, MANUFACTURE AND VARIETIES

A Brief History

As long as there were only a few people sending a limited number of letters, the messengers themselves were able to collect the required postage from all the senders. However, as the amount of post increased people found it very inconvenient to take every letter to a collecting office and pay the postage in cash. As early as the 17th century ways were investigated of marking letters to show that the delivery fee had already been paid, so that post marked to this effect could be simply placed in a box. A solution was already found at the time of the reign of Louis XIV. Senders in Paris could buy small rectangles of paper with the wording *Port payé le ...*, paste the paper on to a letter and place the letter in a collection box.

Louis, who knew perfectly well that his chief minister, Cardinal Mazarin, was checking his personal correspondence, was himself interested to see the novel idea introduced in practice. However, as is often the case with such inventions, the idea was soon forgotten, the rectangles of paper ceased to be sold and postage fees had to be paid once more in cash. Perhaps it is no wonder that the idea did not catch on after all, because the forerunner of the postage stamp interfered with the plans of the powerful Cardinal who conducted France's affrairs.

As time went by the correct calculation of postage became too complicated. It depended on the distance covered by a courier on horseback, the mileage walked by a messenger on foot and the destination to which the letter travelled in the box of a mailcoach. In fact, the exact postage even depended on the number of horses in the mailcoach team. Dissatisfaction with the system was common not only among the customers but also among postmasters themselves because their assistants frequently cheated them and a sizable portion of postal revenues ended up in the wrong hands.

Rowland Hill's design for the world's first postage stamp

Then in the 1830s an Englishman, Rowland Hill, put forward a proposal for the introduction of stamps as we know them today. He even drew the design for the stamps with his own untrained hand, placing a white silhouette of the head of the young Queen Victoria on a black background. Hill justified his proposals in a pamphlet called *Post Office Reform: Its Importance and Practicability*, in which he advocated uniform postage rates based on weight and applicable to the whole of Great Britain regardless of distance. His arguments

Two other entries in the contest for the design of the first stamp

showed that the reform would prove profitable for the Post Office. It cost Hill a lot of effort and much lobbying of influential people before the proposal gained general acceptance. The Post Office then held a public competition for the graphic design of the world's first postage stamp. Although there were more than 2,000 entries, Hill's design was adjudged the best. It was then given to experienced draughtsmen and engravers to work on and in the spring of 1840 the first sheets of stamps were printed and distributed to post offices throughout Britain. The issue became valid on May 6, 1840. On this memorable occasion the world's first postage stamp, or rather first two stamps, saw the light of day. The Post Office issued a black 1 d stamp known as the Penny Black, and a blue version of the same design with the face value of twopence. Neither stamp bore the name of the issuing country. At the time there seemed to be no reason to include this since stamps existed only in Britain. This tradition has been maintained and British issues still give no indication of their country of origin.

It should be perhaps added that Rowland Hill, who later became Postmaster General and was knighted in recognition of his achievements, was the most successful although not the sole inventor of the postage stamp. An English publisher, stationer and printer named Chalmers had proposed the use of postage stamps before Hill did, but he had not been persistent enough to see his idea through. In Austria, the honour of being named the inventor of the postage stamp went to two people, Košír and Eggarter. They arrived at the idea independently of each other and reportedly had done so even before Hill but neither was able to see his proposals adopted. Eggarter, a postmaster, did not wait for an official sanction and is supposed to have introduced stamps at his post office but, unfortunately, he did not leave sufficient proof of what he had done.

The authorities did not even consider his proposal and the records contain only scanty evidence without a single specimen stamp, so that, years later, when a letter bearing the Eggarter stamps was accidentally found, some experts thought them counterfeit. Be that as it may, Austrian catalogues designate the Eggarter stamp as the world's first issue, while everybody else accords the honour to Hill's Penny Black.

At present about 10,000 different issues appear annually world-wide, excluding stamps printed directly on covers, post-cards and other stamped postal stationery. The quantity of each issue differs. There are issues with only a few thousand stamps printed, but there are also stamps that are issued in hundreds of millions.

The Printing of Stamps

Recess (Intaglio) Printing

Recess (intaglio) printing, which is the method employed for printing top-quality stamps, was actually used to manufacture the very first stamps. The process is, however, by no means the most common one. The engraver, using his burin, must incise a mirror image of the stamp design into a steel plate. The engraving must be the actual size, which means that the engraver has to use a magnifying lense constantly and make marks smaller than a quarter of a millimetre in size. Yet even the most experienced of engravers are able to produce only lines and dots with their tools. To engrave shadows or inter-

Impression of a line engraving plate

mediate shades between light and dark is impossible. Areas must be rendered either by dense hatching, i.e. parallel lines running close to each other, or else by densely incised dots. Lights and shadows are obtained by varying the density of the hatching or the dots. When the plate is inked, the ink will penetrate the grooves formed by the incisions, the rest of the plate being wiped clean. Moistened paper is applied to the plate and absorbs the ink from the grooves. When the ink dries it forms a design raised slightly above the paper surface, which can be felt if touched lightly with the finger tips.

In actual printing the process is more complicated and the result much more effective. The engraved steel plate is first hardened and then placed against a soft steel plate. Applying great pressure, the original image from the hardened plate is transferred on to the soft plate, but as a positive image, just the reverse of what is wanted. The soft positive plate is therefore also hardened and the process repeated, this time using a large printing plate rather than a small one. The image is then transferred 50, 100 and even 200 times on to the negative plate. In performing this operation great care must be taken to space the subjects, as the repeated images of the same stamp are called, evenly on the plate. When the printing base is ready, the printing can start.

However, the plate is flat and most printing firms today use rotary printing machines rather than the old-fashioned flat-bed printing presses. The printing plate therefore has to be curved in order to be clamped to the rotary press machine roller. Although the bending force has a tendency to distort the tiny image of the stamp engraving, modern technology has found a way how to cope with this problem too.

If the stamp to be issued is multi-coloured, then a separate engraving and also a printing plate must be made for each colour. To register two or more colours requires great precision, to the order of a hundredth of a millimetre, so that even the printer himself needs a magnifying glass to check on what is being done. It is interesting to note that a skilled engraver can place up to 10,000 incisions on a square centimetre of the area of the stamp. In fact the individual incisions are invisible to the naked eye.

Since intaglio printing is a very exacting task, it is quite expensive and the larger printing firms have stopped using the process. There are, however, several companies, such as Courvoisier in Switzerland, De La Rue in London and state printing offices in Vienna, Paris, Prague and Stockholm, that have had considerable experience with steel engraving and their work has traditionally enjoyed a high reputation among stamp collectors.

Offset Printing

Offset printing is a process used ever more frequently because of its cheapness — it involves practically no work done by hand. The printing surface is a thin metal sheet with the design applied by a special ink. When the printing plate is inked, the ink adheres only to the design while the rest of the surface is wiped clean. From the thin metal sheet the ink is first transferred on to a rubber cylinder against which the cylinder bearing the impression presses the paper. The process can also be used for printing reproductions of colour photography. The resulting print is soft and without sharp outlines. Photographs are

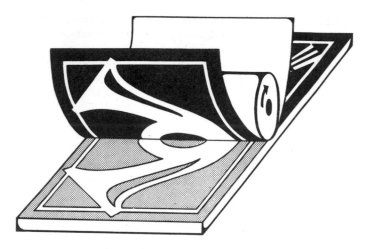

Impression of an offset plate

transferred first on to the metal sheet through a dense mesh of hair known as a screen. This divides the whole photograph into thousands of tiny lighter or darker dots which retain more or less ink during the printing process and thus create intermediate shades between highlights and shadows.

More and more colourful stamps are manufactured today by the offset process which is capable of producing an astonishing range of colours, admired especially in art reproductions. For example, all stamps issued by Arab sheikhdoms are offset printed.

Relief Printing (Typography)

Relief printing is the oldest printing process known to man. The printing surface, whether consisting of letters or wooden, metal, or plastic blocks bearing an image, is raised about one or two millimetres above the rest of the plate.

The process uses autotypes produced by photocopying. A photograph split by a screen into thousands of dots is projected on to a plate treated with an emulsion. The transferred dark spots are stabilized and hardened, and the light spots are etched in depth so that the dark spots are raised and form the printing surfaces. The process is not now used for stamp manufacture but was quite common as late as the end of the 19th and the beginning of the 20th century. Printers did not produce a single printing plate for 100 subjects but laboriously placed 100 identical blocks side by side. From time to time they would by mistake place a block upside down, so that the run produced the so-called tête-bêche, with an inverted stamp alongside, above or below one in the normal position. Or the printer might erroneously include in the plate a block for a different denomination that had been intended for another colour. This then produced a colour error, which, if it passed unnoticed at the inspection stage, was eventually distributed and acquired collector value. If the printer discovered his error in time and replaced the faulty or wrong block with the correct one, the number of errors actually run remained very low and specimens discovered subsequently by philatelists have become priceless rarities. Such was the origin of the most valuable stamp in the world today, the British Guiana 1856 One Cent sold for $ 270,000 at an auction in New York in 1970. Since the face value of the stamp is one cent, it is a fascinating exercise to calculate its percentage price increase in those 114 years, arising from the simple fact that the printer had made a mistake and included a one-cent stamp block in a four-cent stamp plate, but quickly recognized his error and corrected it. Today the British Guiana One Cent is unique because only a single specimen is known to exist. However, the search for high-priced stamps and stamp rarities caused by imperfect work can hardly be considered philately.

Sad to say, the history of stamp manufacture has known a number of such printing errors that have become rarities. The error need not necessarily involve a wrong block in a plate. There are, for example, stamps where the block used for the printing of the centre is inverted in relation to the frame. In the U.S. 24 cents airmail stamp of May 1918, for example, an entire printing sheet was found, in which the picture of the aeroplane in the centre of the stamp was inverted in relation to the frame. When the error was discovered, traders started outbidding each other trying to obtain either the entire sheet or single stamps. The all-time record price for a single stamp was $ 33,000. The price per sheet calculated on this basis would be the astronomical figure of $ 3,333,000. But, again, this has nothing in common with true philately.

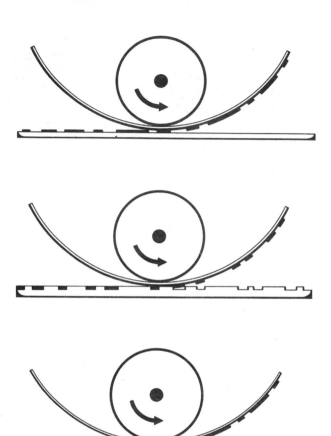

Side views of letterpress, offset and recess printing rollers

Photogravure

This method is usually adopted for rotary printing machines. A photograph divided by a screen into thousands of tiny dots is transferred on to a printing plate and the dark spots are etched, leaving depressions. These depressions are inked while the rest of the plate is wiped clean. A paper pressed against the plate absorbs the ink from the etched dots. Under magnification the image reveals that the print is composed of numerous

Impression of a letterpress block

tiny squares formed by the mesh of the screen. The outlines are therefore less sharp, the printing is characterized by a soft tone and there is less contrast between light and shade.

Embossing

This is a process that uses no ink. There are two plates: on one the image is raised above the surface while the other bears the identical image in sunken relief. When paper is placed between the two plates and pressure is applied, a colourless relief print is produced. The embossed image is either an intaglio or a cameo, depending on the arrangement of the plates. The process was used for the manufacture of some 19th-century Hungarian issues. Today it is used only rarely.

Combined Printing Process

This is often used for stamp manufacture by many postal authorities. Most frequently it combines a single-colour engraving, which produces the outlines of the image, and multi-colour recess printing. Other combinations are also used, for example, the offset and embossing processes. The actual method used for the manufacture of a stamp is usually listed in catalogues.

It is important for the philatelist to become familiar with the various printing processes used in stamp manufacture since there have been — and undoubtedly will be in the future — cases of a stamp printed by several different processes in subsequent runs, for example, first by relief printing or line engraving and then by offset. Although the stamps may have the same design and denomination, they are in fact two different ones: catalogues make a distinction between them and collectors should be able to tell them apart. Besides, their philatelic value may differ and may depend on the quantity produced by each process.

A thorough knowledge of the printing processes is also helpful in the identification of forgeries. If the collector knows — actually he can even find it in a catalogue — that the genuine issue was originally produced by line engraving and he comes across a specimen that has undoubtedly been manufactured by offset or relief printing, he can be quite certain that the latter is a forgery.

Printing Errors and Printer's Waste

Large issues are not usually run from a single printing plate since the plate wears away after some time and must be replaced, or else the plate may be damaged during cleaning, or previously undetected error may be discovered on the original plate, which requires correction. Sometimes a speck of grit adhering to the inked plate will produce a small blotch in a long run. Such stamps will be soon discovered by observant

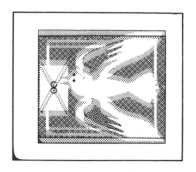

Double impression, basically a reject

philatelists. Similarly, stamp collectors will be quick to recognize even minute corrections on a scratched or otherwise damaged engraving, retouched lines printed too weakly or too strongly, unfinished lines, etc.

A philatelist specializing in an analytical study of an issue must record and document all such errors and flaws in printing. These details can also be helpful in the detection of forgeries. In most cases, however, imperfect printing is caused by careless or negligent work on the part of the printer and, in the author's opinion, there is no reason why shoddy work should be admired, traced and collected by philatelists.

The same goes for the spoilage or printer's waste sheets that are passed two or more times through the press at the beginning of the run to check on the proper inking of the roller. These trial runs have no place in a collection, either, and a conscientious printer will always have such spoilage scrapped. This is to ensure that the waste material does not get outside the premises where it might be offered for large sums of money to inexperienced collectors, who will purchase it in the belief that they are obtaining something of great rarity value.

Apart from the genuine errors mentioned above, this category also includes cases in which the printing sheet passes normally through the machine on the first colour run but sticks to the following sheet on the second run. Such a sheet is then not printed with the second colour and, if it is not detected and scrapped at inspection, it is perforated, counted and ultimately distributed. There have been numerous examples of this in many stamp-issuing countries and stamp dealers seeking large profits have tried to pass the errors off as rarities. The U.S. postal service is famous for its ingenious reaction to such a case. When an imperfect issue lacking one of the colours was discovered, the authorities had more of these specimens printed on purpose. The case developed into a lawsuit because the discoverer of the original faulty sheet sued the service for wilfully obstructing his business. However, he lost his case.

This serves as yet another reminder that philately is not the pursuit of profit or a hunt for printing errors. The overwhelming majority of philatelists pursue their hobby because they appreciate the aesthetic qualities of postage stamps and admire the perfect printing that adds to the beauty of the miniature works of art that they collect.

Materials Used for Stamp Printing

Paper Flaws

All paper intended for use in the manufacture of stamps should be inspected upon delivery at the printing works and all imperfect sheets should be eliminated from the run. However, if the printing is a rush job or is done carelessly, which is usually the case in times of political unrest, in wartime, or when a newly independent state needs its own postage stamp virtually overnight, printers are sometimes forced to use such paper as they have at hand regardless of its quality.

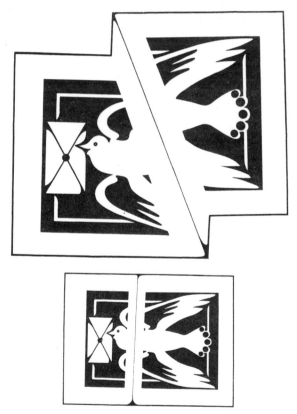

Defects of the printing paper (folds) prior to printing

It may thus happen that a sheet with a folded corner, an imperfectly cut sheet, or one with a centre crease running the entire length of the sheet is fed into the printing press. Each of these imperfections results in numerous production flaws during the printing and the separation of sheets into stamps. A crease that is smoothed out when the stamp is washed and dried will produce branching lines on the design. A corner folded down against the printing face of the paper will produce a stamp with the design printed partially on the gummed, reverse side. If stamps are manufactured by the rotary printing process using a paper web, prints sometimes appear on the splices and stamps printed on this double paper reveal a thicker, darker strip at the joint.

As in the case of printing errors, paper flaws are another imperfection no good printer can be happy about and therefore there is no reason to elevate such variations to the rank of valuable rarities. This applies even if the stamp in question was actually carried by the post, which, in the opinion of some philatelists, constitutes tacit authorization of an imperfect specimen. Such cases actually prove only one thing: that a production fault has been simply followed by improper inspection. When included in a collection such stamps may perhaps be used to document a period when strict quality control slackened. A good example of this is provided by the issues of the Republic of Azerbaijan. Azerbaijan emerged as an independent country at the close of the First World War after the disintegration of Tsarist Russia. The young republic was forced to print its stamp issues on any paper available, on paper of varying basic weight and with any ink that the printers could lay their hands on. The printing presses were operated by women who were often illiterate and worked in cramped basement workshops illuminated by kerosene lamps and filled with the fumes of the petrol engines used to run the machinery. These women operators were mainly concerned with what their meagre wages would buy at the end of the day shift, since the rate of inflation was staggering. It is hardly surprising, then, that they were completely unconcerned about the ink, the quality of the paper and of the printing in general. As a result it is hardly possible to find in 100 stamps, all of which would have been identical under normal conditions, two specimens that would meet the requirement. Although much has been written on these Azerbaijan issues, there is no guarantee that all deviations from the standard have been discovered and recorded yet. A study of such issues is then a valid document for the period in question but no philatelist in his right mind would regard these colour varieties as valuable rarities.

Stamp Paper

Paper used for the manufacture of postage stamps can be used to identify a forgery. A beginner who has by now begun to lose confidence, realizing how many things there are to look for in a stamp, should not be discouraged, however, since it is precisely the purpose of this book to provide essential information that, combined with experience, will in time give him sufficient insight.

Essentially paper is classified according to its thickness, expressed in grams per sheet of a given size. Naturally a philatelist will not weigh his stamps because even the most delicate scales would not be of much help. But even a relative beginner would soon be able to distinguish with his fingers two stamps made from papers of different weight, or in other words, of different thickness. It is sufficient to just bend the stamp a little, holding it between the thumb and two fingers and then let it return to its original position. The thicker the paper, the more springy or elastic it will feel. With a bit of practice, the beginner will be able to make even finer distinctions.

Another important feature of stamp paper is its translucence, although there are stamps printed on unusually thick paper that is totally opaque. If coloured fibres (threads) are left in the paper, the paper shows lay-lines and is designated as laid. Stamps are printed on both wove and laid papers and their market value differs considerably. Basically, laid-paper stamps are less common and therefore tend to be more expensive.

Some stamps are printed on paper with a very smooth surface. These papers are of the coated type and are called art, printed art or chalk paper; the surface is glossy. Poland and the U.S.S.R. have recently started using art paper for stamps, especially those with reproductions of works of art. Art paper, however, is very tricky from the collector's point of view because of its brittleness. The corners of art-paper-printed stamps easily break off and the damage is almost beyond repair or camouflage. Other papers have a smooth, a rough or even a 'bumpy' surface. Such papers are characterized by uneven thickness and, when viewed against light, will reveal 'clouds', i.e., lighter or darker spots caused by the uneven distribution of the paper mass.

Papers come in chalk-white, regular white and greyish- or yellowish-white colour. This, however, does not imply that chalk (art) paper must necessarily be chalk white. The actual colour can be caused either by the character of the paper or it may be the result of the subsequent printing process.

In order to render the forgery of valuable paper more difficult, some paper mills introduced watermarked papers as early as the 13th century. Today, papers with watermarks are used for the manufacture of bank notes and stamps. The watermark is a symbol or image, an initial and sometimes even a complicated ornament, a simple grid or an undulating line that is normally not seen but that can be observed when the paper is viewed against light or immersed in a bath against a black background. According to the distribution, simple watermarks fall on each individual stamp in the sheet while multiple watermarks form a recurrent pattern, each stamp bearing only a part of such a pattern. A typical example of the simple watermark is the monogram of the sovereign used on British issues, the letter **R** standing for the Latin *Rex* ('king') or *Regina* ('queen').

Stamp paper watermarks from various countries

Watermarks of German stamps issued in the 1930s can serve as an identification mark for the individual issues of the same stamp, which may otherwise seem identical at first glance.

Stamp paper watermarks

Stamp paper watermarks from various countries

A typical example would be the Hindenburg issue which comes with either a rhomboid grille or a swastika watermark. When looking for the watermark of a stamp it is sometimes sufficient to tilt the reverse of the stamp at an angle under light. In cancelled stamps with the gum washed off a small droplet of water can be used, while a benzine bath and a black tray are used for mint stamps with the gum intact. The latter method should not be repeated too often on a single specimen because the gum could be damaged, and the benzine could even affect the colour of some issues, although this danger is usually noted in major catalogues. To look for a watermark on a stamp affixed to a cover is very difficult, but can be achieved by patiently tilting the cover backwards and forwards against the light.

Fluorescent Paper

Fluorescent paper uses agents that cause cold-light emission if the paper is illuminated by ultrashort light wave frequencies, for example ultraviolet light. Stamps printed on fluorescent paper are more difficult to counterfeit, but their major advantage is that they permit the automatic sorting of mail. A cancelling machine equipped with a photocell will always identify the stamp because this emits a yellowish-orange light when illuminated, while the rest of the cover remains black. Stamps printed on fluorescent paper have been issued in Italy, Denmark, Switzerland, and the Federal Republic of Germany, and experiments with fluorescent paper stamps have also been carried out in other countries. Collectors can distinguish such stamps with a quartz lamp emitting ultraviolet light.

Luminescent agents are also in quality paper used, for the manufacture of letter paper and envelopes. These agents have a strong bleaching effect and give the paper a dazzling white colour. It is important for a philatelist to remember that luminescent papers may leave marks on album paper if the stamp remains stuck in one place for a long time. The problem is that the emissions penetrate the paper and may affect stamps attached to the reverse side of the page. It is therefore advisable to lay parchmentized paper between album sheets with stamps printed on luminescent paper. It should also be noted that the luminescence becomes weaker in time and may even disappear altogether.

Silk Fabric

This was used in 1968 in Poland for a block issued to commemorate the 400th anniversary of the Polish postal service.

Dederon Fabric

This was used for a special block issued by the German Democratic Republic in 1963 to mark the achievements of the country's chemical industry. Dederon (the name is derived from the German abbreviation of the country's name, DDR) is a nylon-type material produced chemically from coal.

Aluminium Foil

Metal foil used for stamp printing is usually very thin. Its gauge including the paper backing (if there is one) is less than .5 of a millimetre. The first postage stamp printed on aluminium foil was manufactured in Hungary in 1955 to commemorate the 20th anniversary of the Hungarian aluminium industry. The flexible foil used for the stamp was .009 mm thick.

Steel Foil

This type of material was first used in Bhutan in 1969 for a stamp marking the achievements of the country's steel industry. The foil was .025 mm thick and the entire issue consisted of eight specimens.

Gold Foil

Gold foil with a paper backing was used for the first time for stamp printing by the Kingdom of Tonga. The stamps were round and embossed and looked rather like thin coins. They served to mark the issue of the first Polynesian gold coinage. The face value of this 1963 issue was very high to provide sufficient receipts in order to cover the cost of the material used and to capitalize on a novel idea. Two years later the Republic of Gabon issued a gold foil stamp without a paper backing to commemorate Albert Schweitzer. The stamps were widely acclaimed and several other countries followed suit and printed stamps on gold foil, both with and without a paper backing. By 1972 ten countries, among them Arab emirates, had issued stamps in gold foil. Needless to say, the decision to issue such stamps was dictated by the desire to acquire huge profits from sales orientated towards the philatelist market, the tourists and curio seekers, rather than by the genuine needs of the postal services.

All metal or fabric stamps issued so far have had gum on the reverse side but, whereas cheap fabric or aluminium stamps were normally used in the mail, a letter bearing a gold foil stamp with a high face value which has been handled by the postal authorities is a rarity.

Stamps with Luminescent Lines

Rather than tagging the stamp paper with luminescent agents some authorities prefer to use luminescent printing inks for their stamps, or stamps covered with a layer of some transparent varnish with a luminescent agent included. Regardless of the type of application of these agents, the use of luminescent materials is always governed by the needs of automatically facing, handling and cancelling mail. For example, Britain has issued identical stamps with and without tag lines.

Stamp Gum

Different printing firms naturally use different adhesives — called gum by philatelists. Only philatelists are aware that the ease with which gum may be removed from cancelled stamps varies considerably. For instance, to wash the gum off some Austro-Hungarian issues is nearly impossible, whereas the gum used in contemporary issues can be removed relatively easily, and it is usually sufficient to let the piece of the backing bearing the stamp soak for a few minutes in lukewarm water.

Gums range in hue from the virtually colourless to yellowish or even brownish. The gum may be either glossy or matt in appearance. Stamps intended for use in the tropics have special gums that prevent entire sheets from sticking together as a result of the combination of temperature and humidity. Gums may be striped, grille-shaped, smooth, grainy, bubbly or patterned, for example, in the form of monograms. Striping, whether horizontal or vertical, is produced in the dryer attached to the rotary gum applicator and used to permit the immediate cutting of the paper web into sheets.

Following the Second World War the philatelic world began insisting that only unused stamps in top condition with the gum intact should be used for collections. In an effort to push up the prices of stamps they marketed to as high a level as possible, stamp dealers started listing three price columns rather than two as customary before: used; unused — no gum; and mint. The last term was used to designate unused stamps with the original gum intact and without any trace of having ever been mounted in a collection, i.e. without a remnant of an adhesive paper hinge. Many collectors ceased evaluating stamps on the merits of their design and concentrated on the condition of the gum instead. In fact they could be said to be collecting mainly gum. The artificiality of the demand for mint condition stamps can be judged from the host of articles on the subject that appeared in the philatelic press, but mainly from the fact that it is practically impossible nowadays to find classic issues with the gum intact. Yet no one would dare to say that these classic issues that have survived many years in perfect condition mounted on a hinge in an album are simply inferior in quality because they are not mint.

Separation

The first stamps were distributed to post offices in whole sheets and when a postal clerk had to sell a stamp or two to a customer, he simply took a pair of scissors and cut the required number from the sheet. Scissors were in fact an indispensable tool for every postal clerk in all those countries that introduced postage stamps in the mid-19th century. Printers kept this in mind and made sure that enough free space or margin was left around each subject in the sheet to permit the clerk to cut the stamp out without having to hold his breath at the same time. Nobody realized that one day stamps would be scrutinized by philatelists armed with magnifying lenses to determine if the margin was wide enough and if the postal clerk working at great speed had not cut into the 'body' (design) of the stamp. Nor could anyone have possibly foreseen that collectors would become annoyed if they happened to come across a specimen with unusually wide margins, not realizing of course that all those stamps adjacent to their prized discovery must have been cheated of their rightful margin. Strange as it may seem, a wide margin in imperforate stamps is highly valued by philatelists.

Soon both the postal clerks and the waiting customers realized that the separation of stamps from sheets by means of scissors was a rather lengthy business and clever minds decided to tackle the problem. It was a certain Henry Archer who came up with a solution, a primitive perforation machine producing stamps that could be easily and quickly separated from the printing sheet. Although the British Post Office put his invention to use quickly enough, it was in no hurry to reward him for his enterprise, refusing to concede that the Archer perforator was a revolutionary idea that was to save a lot of time. It took Archer two years before the Post Office finally dipped into its purse but even then the paltry sum was more of a consolation prize of the kind usually paid for minor improvements.

These events took place ten years after the introduction of the first postage stamp. Meanwhile, there were other countries that could now boast of stamps of their own. In Germany, at that time divided into a number of independent states, principalities and free cities, perforation was used first in 1860 when Baden and Württemberg pooled their resources and jointly purchased a perforation machine. However, the machine could not be installed at the border between the two principalities, especially since the princely house of Thurn-Taxis also claimed the right to use it as they too had contributed. After protracted negotiations it was decided that the new machine would be installed in Karlsruhe, in the territory of the Grand Duchy of Baden. The officials in Baden gave priority to their jobs and, since the machine was rather faulty and had to be repaired frequently, it was not surprising that their partners could not always wait and their perforated issues were frequently followed by imperforate ones. This is yet another example of the slow and painful advance of technology, especially in countries that had started introducing gummed postage stamps at about that time. And so the most expensive stamp of the world, the British Guiana One Cent Red, issued in 1856, several years after Britain, the country of origin of the postage stamp, had started using perforation machines, is imperforate, and even has all four corners cut off, making it really an octagon.

Single-Line Perforation

Perforation is the most commonly used but not the sole method of stamp separation. In single-line perforation the perforation machine consists of a row of pins arranged in a line known as the perforation bar. A sheet of stamps is fed into the machine and a first row of holes is punched along the outside margin of the stamps. The sheet is then pushed further in by the width of one stamp and the bar punches another perforation line until all lines are perforated. The sheet is then rotated 90 degrees and new perforation lines are punched perpendicular to the original

Line perforation

ones. The process is quite slow, however, and somewhat imprecise, so that where the vertical and horizontal lines meet the corners of the stamps are often cut off.

Comb Perforation

In this operation the perforation comb punches perforations on three sides of each row of stamps. This prevents the corners of stamps from being damaged and it is not necessary to turn

Comb perforation

the sheet 90 degrees and run it again through the perforator, which operates both vertically and horizontally. The comb may sometimes strike slightly off centre and stamps of one row may be somewhat larger than those of the next.

Harrow Perforation

Harrow perforation machines, which punch whole sheets at a single stroke, are generally used on smaller sheets of stamps.

Harrow perforation

Compound Perforation

This kind of perforation is sometimes used by printing offices for technical reasons, combining, for example, line and harrow perforation.

The perforation pins may of course differ in thickness and, consequently, the perforations they produce. The perforations are easy to measure with a perforation gauge available in philatelic shops. It is very important for the philatelist to know stamp perforations since printing offices are sometimes obliged to use different machines for the perforation of a single issue and some gauges may become rarer, which naturally affects the price of the stamp in question. In practice, however, only specialists who document issues of a particular country in great detail study perforations thoroughly. Topical collectors are usually satisfied with the observation that the perforation of their stamp is intact.

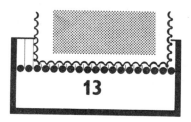

Gauging a perforation

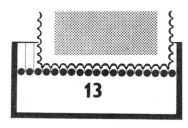

Gauging a perforation when the teeth do not correspond to the scale

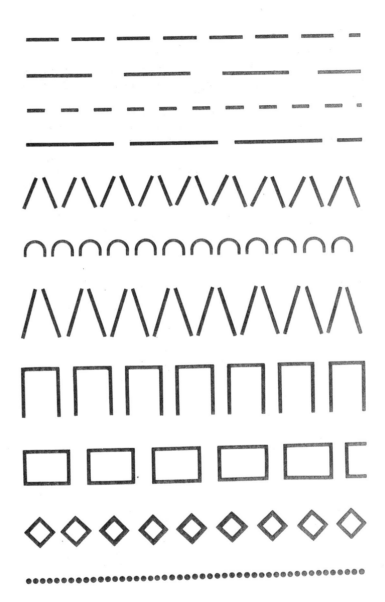

Various types of rouletting

Rouletting

Rouletting is a type of stamp separation process using short knives or blades to cut the paper. The method was frequently used by the old German states, notably by the Thurn-Taxis post. The separated stamps show no perforation but margins clearly reveal where the paper was punched and where it had to be torn off.

Pin Rouletting

Known in English (somewhat incorrectly) as pin perforation, and in French as *percé en points*, this uses relatively thin, sharp-pointed pins which prick holes but do not actually cut out paper, and the separated stamp consequently does not reveal the characteristic perforation indentations. The method was used for separation of some late-19th century private German local issues.

Perforation of stamps sold in booklets

Perforation of stamps sold in vending machines

Coil Stamps

To expedite the handling of stamps at post office counters and to facilitate stamp sales by vending machines, parts of an issue may be manufactured in the form of long strips or coils so that two sides of each stamp are cut (imperforate) and two are perforated to make the separation from the stamp coil easier. A similar combination is used for the stamp booklets that are sold in many countries. It would be erroneous to think, for instance, that a U.S. stamp with two imperforate sides is a damaged specimen. Coil and booklet stamps have become very common, for example, in Sweden and Swedish catalogues even list perforation varieties that can be collected: ordinary perforated stamps, i.e., perforated on all four sides, those with three sides perforated and the fourth imperforate either at the top or at the bottom, i.e., stamps marketed in booklet form, or coil stamps with two perforated and two imperforated sides. The number of each variety issued determines the difference in price in the catalogue.

Perforation Errors and Flaws

No human activity can be exempt from errors and therefore unintentional mistakes can occur during the perforation of sheets of stamps. For example, if a sheet is fed into the machine

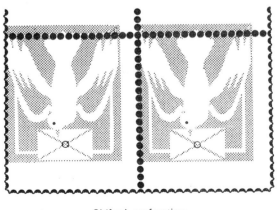

Shifted perforation

a millimetre or two too far and a row of stamps is left without a margin when the perforation bar strikes, or if the perforation bar punches the design, the opposite margin will be too wide. As a result, the centre is wrongly aligned and the aesthetic quality and the appeal of the stamp are spoiled. When line perforators are used, the bar may strike a few millimetres short of the correct position. When the sheet is subsequently straightened and the bar strikes again, this time in the correct position, the stamp will have a detachable tag with a part of the design on it. Although these specimens with double perforations should be scrapped at the inspection stage, there are collectors who are on the lookout for such flaws and are willing to pay good money for them. A true philatelist, however, should take them for what they are — production errors rather than rarities to be sought after.

Stamp Colours

The designer of a stamp, or the engraver, together with a post office official stipulate the precise colour chart to be used for each issue and the company printing the stamps is expected to adhere to the chart in subsequent runs. This, however, is not easy. In wintertime, in particular, when artificial light is used for illumination, colours may often be mixed differently in spite of all precautions on the part of the printer, or the fault may lie with the ink manufacturer, who delivers a different shade under the same code number. The colour change may also be caused by a paper of different quality used in subsequent runs.

Philatelists specializing in a territory regard colour flaws as welcome variations that help them to document such things as the number of reissues or the popularity and period of validity of the stamp. Some issues with especially pronounced colour variations are listed in catalogues and the individual colour varieties are separately priced. The designation of colour in catalogues may sometimes cause problems because a stamp identified by one catalogue as bright red may be in fact identical with the same stamp designated elsewhere as orange. If you are not able to compare your stamp against the whole set of colour varieties, it is best to seek the advice of an expert specializing in the territory in question.

The world's first stamp, the Penny Black, was printed in sheets of 240 subjects. The unusual number of stamps per

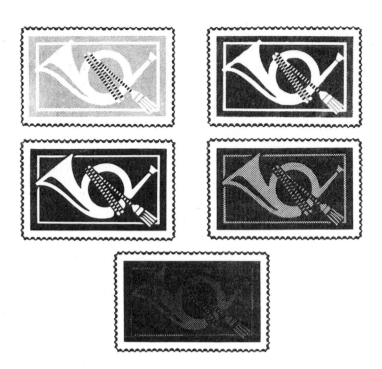

Different shades of the same colour used in subsequent printing runs

sheet was governed by the British currency system. A pound
had 20 shillings and each shilling consisted of 12 pence.
A whole sheet of Penny Blacks therefore cost one pound,
while a sheet of Twopenny Blues was worth twice as much.
Posts in countries using decimal monetary systems naturally
adjusted the number of stamps on a sheet to their currency,
the sheets usually having 100 or 200 subjects.

However, since the handling of large sheets at post office
counters would prove rather awkward, there are also the
so-called counter or post office sheets (also known as panes)
comprising usually half the total number of subjects in the
sheet. Printers take this into account during plating, and, to
facilitate the cutting of sheets in half prior to distribution, they
print the counter sheets with blank white margins known as
gutters, or print commercial advertisements on them. The
gutters are sometimes perforated with the rest of the printing

sheet. Occasionally they are left imperforate. Why this is important for philatelists will be revealed in subsequent chapters.

Plating and Position of the Stamp in the Printing Sheet

As explained above, the postal authorities tried to adjust the number of subjects per sheet in such a way as to make the total value of all stamps in the sheet a round sum, e.g., one hundred francs, crowns or marks. If the denominations of the stamps were in whole units, that is, without decimal fractions, the round sum was relatively easy to make up, but not so in case of small denominations. A few subjects had to be sometimes omitted from the sheet and the empty spaces were printed with diagonal crosses. These crosses, the so-called St Andrew's Crosses, were usually printed in a conspicuous colour used for the design. They appear frequently on the sheets of Austrian Imperial issues and those of the Kingdom of Bavaria and others. In Germany, the crosses remained in use long after the First World War.

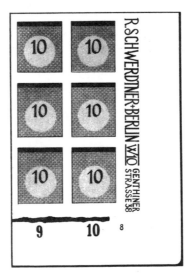

Stamp printing sheet margin

Tabs

Originally, those spaces on the sheet that were either blank or printed with St Andrew's Crosses, were grouped side by side at the bottom of the sheet. The spaces themselves have no signifi-

St Andrew's Cross

Stamp with a right tab

cance and no philatelic value but, when attached to the adjacent stamp, they serve as an example of the stamp sheet and philatelists seek to include them in their collections.

In time some postal authorities decided that the aesthetic appeal of commemorative and special issues would be enhanced if the empty spaces or 'fields' in a printing sheet formed a whole with the adjacent stamps. The blank area was printed with a symbolic design and the so-called tab came into being. Since these tabs met with great approval among philatelists, printing sheets were made with still greater numbers of them. Later on sheets of issues marking major philatelic exhibitions

Stamp with a left tab

Stamp with a top tab

Stamp with a bottom tab

had as many tabs as they had stamps. As a result, catalogues reacted to the popularity of tabs and ascribed to them a varying philatelic value, with different prices quoted for stamps having right, left, top or bottom tabs.

Publicity-seeking business companies purchased tabs in large quantities for their advertisements, which were usually printed on tabs in stamp booklets containing stamps run off from the original printing plates but with larger margins around them. Booklets usually contained five or ten of each of the two most common denominations used for the domestic post. Before the Second World War the French postal authorities had a huge quantity of such booklets printed in advance and then waited for business companies to buy them and have them printed with their advertisements. Such speculative issues are also listed in catalogues and their price may be quite high in some cases. For example, some early 20th-century Bavarian and German issues, nominally only of low denomination, fetch up to several hundred Deutsche Marks on the market nowadays if they have some advertisement tabs attached.

Tab with printed text

Another case from the history of philately involves a deal made between a pharmaceutical manufacturer and the French postal authorities for the use of tabs in booklet issues of a popular stamp bearing the symbol of France, the Sowing Maid. Neither of the parties to the agreement realized that the booklets were reissued from newly engraved plates. Philatelists, however, soon discovered that the text was set in a different type and the stamps were suddenly in great demand. The drug company recognized a great opportunity for more business and, instead of giving the booklets away as courtesy promotion gifts, it started to insert single specimens of the popular issue at random in boxes with small amounts of one of their products, which soon sold out completely.

A similar case from France concerned a cheese advertisement with the slogan *La vache qui rit* ('The cow that smiles') printed on tabs of stamps bearing the image of Joan of Arc. Since the French revere Joan of Arc as a national saint, the case caused a great outrage, although there was hardly a French man or woman who would not have been familiar with the brand of cheese in question.

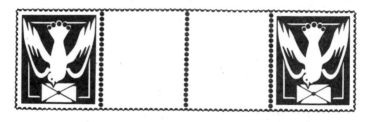

Gutter

Gutters

The empty strips of paper dividing two counter sheets, usually the width of two or three stamps and divided by perforations into the same number of spaces or 'fields', are called gutters by philatelists. Naturally the latter do not collect these empty spaces alone but gutters with one or two subjects attached to each side. Moreover, since the printing firms generally utilize sheet margins to record their pure, i.e. non-registered colours, many gutters bear narrow colour bands.

Gutter Crosses

These are quite rare since they appear only on printing sheets containing four counter sheets separated by wide, unprinted gutters. The cross is formed when the corner stamps of each counter sheet and the adjacent intersection of the horizontal and vertical gutters are cut out as a whole (small cross), or four subjects from the corner of each counter sheet and the two gutters (large cross). A small cross consists, then, of four subjects and the large one of sixteen. A good example is the 1945 Czechoslovak Košice issue.

Tête-Bêche

The two counter sheets are sometimes printed inverted in relation to each other in the printing sheet. At the line where the two counter sheets meet, tête-bêches (pairs of stamps in which one of the subjects is upside down in relation to the other) are found in rows. The two stamps may also be separated by a gutter. Tête-bêches are also frequently found in stamp booklets and are appreciated and collected, especially by territorialists.

Tête-bêche

Se-tenant Stamps

Se-tenant stamps, another type prized by philatelists, are two or more different stamps that appear together in one sheet, block or booklet. The stamps may differ in denomination, colour and design. Se-tenant stamps are frequently found in booklets containing stamps of the most commonly used denominations. Apart from that, se-tenant stamps are printed to mark major international philatelic exhibitions and important national events. The se-tenant pairs may be horizontal, vertical or they may constitute tête-bêches.

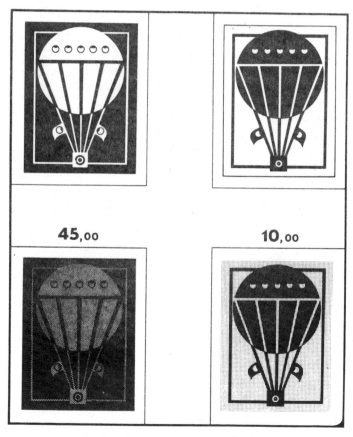

Four stamp gutter cross

Se-tenants in a coil

Se-tenants in a miniature sheet

False Tabs — Sheet Margins

Sheet margins remain only rarely unprinted because commercial companies often pay the postal authorities for permission to use them for advertisement purposes. Even the Post Office itself finds a use for the margins, especially for the inclusion of various practical data that make the work of counter clerks and accountants easier. Among these items are, for instance, the totals of all the nominal values in a column. The totals are sometimes printed on both the top and the bottom margins of the sheet. Sometimes one margin carries the totals and the other the column numbers. Each row is marked with a number representing partial totals of subjects. The printers also find the margin a handy place on which to mark their imprint, the job number, colour scheme, plate numbers and various other data. Some of these data, for example the plate numbers, are of interest to the collector, too.

Plate mark imprint in a printing sheet corner

Unprinted sheet margins have been often used for the printing of forgeries. In order to prevent such misuse of margins, paper mills sometimes produce margins with watermarks that differ from those used in the stamp field.

False tabs, however, do not constitute forgeries. Such tabs are formed when the perforating machine also punctures sheet margins which should have been left untouched. In this way, each margin stamp has a piece attached at the side, the top or the bottom. The attachment may be either white and blank, or printed. It is, however, not intended as a tab. If it is printed,

False tab (printing sheet margin)

it may carry only a fragment of a word or slogan which has no meaning because it is incomplete. The same applies to the graphic design An attachment like this is usually smaller in size than a regular tab. Philatelists do not separate the stamps from these attachments needlessly, since they may contain important bits of information. In a few cases, they are registered in catalogues and priced.

Miniature (Souvenir) Sheets

These are philatelic material issued usually to mark an important national event. A stamp, or possibly an entire set, is printed separately on a small sheet of paper in such a way as to leave a free margin around the stamp or stamps. In some cases the field surrounding the stamps is left blank because the stamps in themselves indicate the reason for the issue. In other cases the field is printed with a slogan, a design or both. The stamps

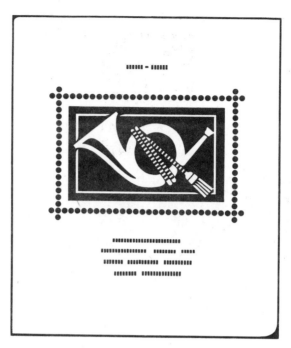

Miniature sheet with a single subject and a text

in a miniature sheet or block may be delineated by perforation but this need not always be so. Some authorities permit stamps to be cut from miniature sheets and used for postage, or authorize the use of the entire miniature sheet for such purposes. However, there are also purely commemorative sheets that have no value as postage. Many miniature sheets are numbered, although again, there is no rule about this. A numbered sheet of this sort simply means that the issue is quite limited and that the sheet has a philatelic value. Such issues are quite frequently put out by the Soviet postal authorities. Generally speaking, miniature sheets are distributed in much smaller quantities than ordinary stamps of the same issue.

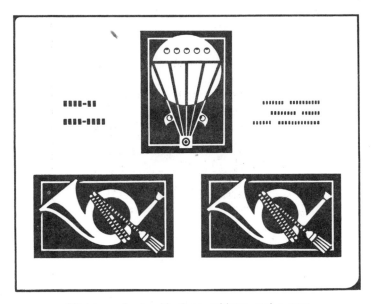

Miniature sheet with three subjects and a text

Small Printing Sheets

Unlike miniature sheets, small printing sheets are intended for separation into individual stamps and are used for postage. The stamps are generally of the same design and face value. Small printing sheets are used for high denominations that are sold only in small quantities, or when unusual printing processes are employed for the manufacture of the issue.

There are collectors who include intact sheets of this kind in their collections and some even believe that the value of their collection will increase with the addition of such material. This is a mistake, however, because from the philatelic point of view small printing sheets have no special value, especially if unused. On the other hand, a cancelled small printing sheet on an entire or a cut-square, i.e. one that has been used postally, has a certain collector's value as a document of unusual franking. It should, however, reflect the usual rates and meet postal regulations.

Black Proofs

Before a new stamp is printed, many printers run proofs of autotypes or entire printing plates in black only, usually at the request of the issuing agency. These black proofs represent an authentic sample of the stamp design, and are of a much better quality than mere photographs of printing bases. Some authorities use black proofs to promote the new issue and send them to editors to be reprinted in the philatelic press. Since black proofs are usually run in limited quantities and since they constitute authorized prints of engravings, they are quite popular among collectors and catalogues list their prices.

Somewhat different is the situation regarding black proofs which are permitted by the authorities to be used as promotional supplements to various professional publications. In some cases black proofs appear as supplements to catalogues of major international philatelic exhibitions. Unlike black proofs for use by the press, these prints usually appear as miniature sheets on white paper, sometimes even accompanied by an explanatory note giving the reason for the issue and often also numbered.

The third reason why black proofs are printed are the so-called favour prints. These black proofs in a miniature sheet form are intended as gifts and souvenirs for high-ranking officials and others whose assistance is especially appreciated. In spite of their name, black proofs can also be printed in other colours.

Printed Matter on the Reverse

Although not very frequent, printed matter is sometimes found on the reverse of modern issues. This supplements or explains the data found on the face. For instance, in 1971 Nicaragua issued a set of stamps featuring portraits of world-famous soccer players, with their names, countries, clubs and number of matches played printed on the reverse.

This, however, does not mean that the reverse of classic issues was always left blank. For example, the 1880 New Zealand issue bears names of various business companies on the reverse, often with their advertising slogans and offers of service. In 1879 Württemberg had the reverse of one of its issues printed with a note stating that the issue was not for sale and was to be used only for official purposes.

Stamps with text on the back

In 1921 the public in western Hungary could buy stamps, the reverse of which bore a notice that a 50 % surtax had to be added to the face value when the stamp was sold. Receipts from the sales were earmarked for the army high command.

Nominal (Face) Value

The nominal value actually does not mean the price of the stamp itself but the price of the service that the post office guarantees to render when the stamp is submitted duly affixed. In other words, any stamp is a kind of a letter of credit that will be reimbursed in the form of service when presented. According to the regulations of the Universal Postal Convention the face value of a stamp must always be expressed in Arabic numerals. Apart from that, the numerals employed in the country of issue may be used. In case of stamps carrying a surtax, regardless of the beneficiary, it must be absolutely clear from the design and layout which is the postage proper and which is the surtax. The two usually differ in the size of the numerals used, those indicating the postage being larger. The Convention does not stipulate that the currency be specified after the numerals because it is presumed that the currency is that of the issuing country. There are also stamps without any face value designation. For instance, the price of certain stamps

Stamp with a surtax of 50 % of the face value

issued by Great Britain for some of its dependencies in the Indian Ocean was governed by colour and local custom, and a stamp of the same colour could have a different value in another territory.

Reprints

A reprint is a new print from the original engraving, autotype or an entire printing plate after the issue of the particular stamp has been discontinued. Reprints differ from black proofs by being printed in the original colours and with the same layout as the original issue. However, a reprint has no value as postage although it is officially authorized and made on the express order of the authorities. Reprints are used solely as souvenirs. Since these issues are usually quite popular and therefore have a collector value, the reprint is usually done on a different paper from that of the original issue to eliminate the possibility of the two being confused. Sometimes the date and the accompanying note are printed on the reverse. For example, on the occasion of the WIPA 1965 Exhibition the Austrian Post Office issued a commemorative reprint of a much-valued special stamp issued originally to mark the WIPA 1933 Exhibition. Although the reprint was black, i.e. in a different colour from that of the original issue, and appeared as an imperforate single on a miniature sheet, the Austrians still deemed it necessary to add a notice that the stamp was a reprint.

Overprints

An overprint is usually a separately typecast and printed abbreviation, word or slogan with which an already issued stamp is imprinted. An overprint must not alter the face value or type of the stamp. In other words, it must not change an ordinary postage stamp into a postage due stamp, nor is it allowed to change the country or other essential characteristics of the stamp to which it is applied. Overprints are usually made to mark various important national and international events, such as manned spaceflights, major philatelic exhibitions, world congresses, important sport events, etc. Overprints may be either official or private although the latter are also authorized by the postal authorities. Overprints that have been made without such authorization or even against an express order have no place in a collection.

Overprinted stamp

Surcharges

Surcharges are overprints applied to a finished stamp that change its original character. For example they may transform postage stamps into official (service) or airmail stamps, or alter their face value or even their country. The surcharge can be composed of words or symbols signifying that the stamp is to be used as an official stamp, or possibly a picture of an aircraft that will change a surface mail stamp into an airmail one. An interesting example of surchage is the 1947 issue of the all-German post overprinted in 1948 with a band featuring a postal horn or a recurrent postal horn pattern. The surcharge in fact changed the country of the stamp because the issue was to be

Surcharge altering the character of the stamp

used exclusively in the U.S. and British occupation zones. Since surcharges always represent a makeshift solution, the printing is done in a hurry and it is therefore only natural that there are many errors, notably misaligned and inverted overprints, double impressions, etc. In the issue mentioned above

Example of a poor printing job: double surcharge, one even inverted

some inverted overprints were made. However, a postal horn printed upside down is not as conspicuous as, say, an inverted text. For instance, the old Austrian Imperial Eagle 4 crown issue was surcharged in 1919 with the text *POŠTA ČESKOSLO-VENSKÁ 1919* ('Czechoslovak Post'), converting the stamp into the issue of the successor state. The surcharge is inverted on a single specimen which has become a unique rarity.

Like overprints, surcharges can be either official or semi-official. Semi-official ones were authorized by a local or regional administration for their territory without the approval of the head office. Among such stamps belong various early 20th-century surcharges issued by regional administrations for the benefit of the then emerging airlines. There are also many private surcharges that were accepted for handling by the post office only as a result of an oversight on the part of postal clerks, e.g., all the known surcharged issues of the former Protectorate of Bohemia and Moravia (in German *Protektorat Böhmen und Mähren*) that appeared in 1945 in various Czechoslovak cities and towns, often on the direct orders of local postmasters.

The surcharges were made against the express command of the postal administration, since the Czechoslovak government in exile had had new Czechoslovak issues printed in London and Moscow long before the war ended and had already started distributing them in the liberated territories. These privately surcharged stamps were, nevertheless, in some cases accepted by local post offices, and mail with these postage stamps was actually delivered. If unused, such private surcharges represent mere worthless labels that could have been made in large numbers by anybody but, if they appear on a cover or an entire, which means that the article was actually accepted for handling, they may be included in a collection as an interesting period document.

Specimens

Some postal authorities send actual stamps rather than mere photographs or black proofs to philatelic journalists before the issue is validated for use. In order to prevent them being misused or passed as undesirable rarities, the Post Office invalidates them with an overprint at the bottom, usually a warning that the stamp must not be used for postage. At one time the British Post Office distributed specimens of new issues including a leaflet with the relevant data cast in plexiglass blocks.

The methods devised to prevent the misuse of specimens, issued in advance to journalists, are numerous, but some curious cases of misuse or speculation have been recorded in several countries. After the death of the West German Chancellor, Konrad Adenauer, the German Bundespost decided to honour the deceased statesman with an issue bearing his portrait. The

Stamp specimens used for promotion of a new issue

stamp was of a denomination that had been traditionally red. The new red stamp overprinted with the word *Muster* ('specimen') was distributed widely among editors and journalists of the philatelic press both in West Germany and in other countries. Soon, however, critical voices were heard protesting at the association of the red, the colour of Communism, with Adenauer, who had been known as a sworn enemy of that political philosophy. A 'Red Adenauer' issue turned out to be a political blunder. The embarrassed Bundespost decided to reprint the stamp in a different colour and asked all persons and organizations on their mailing list to return the specimens of the red issue. The majority obliged but some people ignored the request and years later these privately held specimens appeared on the philatelic market as highly valued rarities.

Unissued Stamps

It sometimes happens — and, in fact, all stamp-issuing authorities are liable to experience this sooner or later — that a postal administration has a stamp printed but decides prior to the definitive validation, announcement in the postal gazette and distribution to post offices, that the new issue is not to be used for some reason or other. The whole issue is then scrapped in a paper mill under the supervision of an official authority and the matter is closed. However, since there is always a certain delay between the printing and the scrapping, some stamps will reach the philatelic market regardless of security measures. There are always people who are willing to pay a lot of money for such stamps although they never have been and never will be official. One should bear in mind that these stamps are invariably stolen and the issuing country considers the possession of them as a violation of its laws. Although such stamps are frequently circulated only after the limitation of the offence, these miniature prints — because that is what they really are — have nothing in common with philately.

Perfins

Many companies laid a stock of stamps and provided them with perfins to prevent company personnel from misusing them.

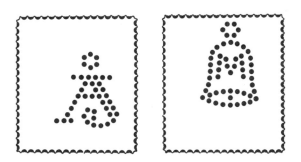

Company perfin to prevent unauthorized use of stamps by company personnel

This type of stamp marking was used also officially in the past; for instance in Bavaria it was used to change postage stamps into official (service) stamps in 1912—15

So-called POL perfin used by German police to mark stamps for police use and very popular among philatelists today

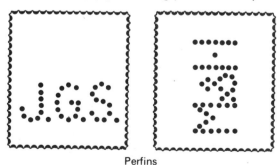

Perfins

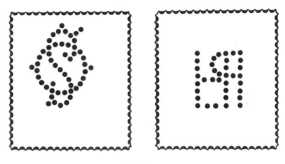

Perfins

STAMPS AS VISITING CARDS

The volume of mail handled by the post has been steadily growing ever since the introduction of Rowland Hill's invention and in
time the small adhesive paper labels certifying that postage has
been paid have also acquired other than purely postal functions.
This book cannot deal with all of them but least one should be
mentioned here. Throughout the world stamps have become
representatives or visiting cards, if you will, of the country of
issue. These little pictures promote the country's natural
beauty, commemorate interesting facts about its past, show
outstanding works of art in its museums and galleries, advertise
major sporting events, etc. The postage stamp, this great work
of art in miniature, serves its country as a perfect ambassador.
Untold millions of collectors all over the world take stamps
carefully in their hands, scrutinize them, note the facts recorded
by them, appreciate their aesthetic appeal and decide whether
to include them in their collections or to trade them for other
stamps. People in public relations have long been aware that
no leaflet or promotion brochure is handled so frequently and
observed so carefully by so many as these little state visiting
cards that cross international borders oblivious of differences
of language, religion or politics.

What is important for the collector, however, are the paths
that these cards follow to reach their destinations. This modern
age has devised a number of means of transport whose name
is also applied to stamps. Not all authorities employ every type
of stamp in existence and some types are even obsolete, yet

philatelists still value them as postal documents of stamp-issuing countries.

Postage Stamps

Each stamp-issuing country continually produces basic sets of standard stamps printed in huge quantities, usually as multiple prints intended to remain in use for a number of years. Such sets must include all denominations that are used for payment of the usual postal rates and can be combined to make up all the higher values that may be required. Standard stamps issued in large sets provide philatelists with a lot of material for the study of colour varieties, printing errors, paper and perforation flaws, retouches, plate numbers, etc.

Airmail Stamps

These are usually of higher face value and the basic set may remain valid for a number of years. In the early days of airmail special airmail stamps were rarely to be found in an average collection since mail were not very often carried by air and airmail stamps therefore represented top-value exhibits. However, as the volume of airmail grew, the postal authorities came to accept airmail with regular postage stamps. After the Second World War the practice of issuing special airmail stamps was gradually discontinued, although from time to time some authorities, as, for example, the U.S. Mails, still issue special airmail stamps. It interesting to note that many postal authorities even carry regular surface mail that has not been prepaid for airmail by aircraft on inland or continental routes. As a rule, however, special airmail postage is nowadays required for overseas mail.

Railway Stamps

As both an important partner and a competitor, the railway also handles and carries mail independently of the post office and many countries have, therefore, issued special railway stamps. The best-known issues of this kind are Belgian, as this country still continues the practice.

The history of postal services includes a very interesting

case of a short railway carriage for mail, for which special postage stamps were devised. The stamps were issues of a privately owned business that established the route and operated it for some time. The stamps bore the letters DBSR. The initials do not stand for the name of any particular country. The DBSR stamps originated in the mid-19th century when the map of Europe looked very different from what it does today. The Balkan countries were divided into many principalities dependent to a greater or lesser extent on Turkey. At that time Turkey also ruled Bulgaria and the emerging principality of Romania.

Constanta, today a booming Romanian seaport, was then known as Küstendje. Located near the Danubian delta, it soon became a major cargo-handling centre. Most central European shipments to the Balkans and the Black Sea ports were handled by the Danubian Steam Ship Company, an Austrian venture. However, the Imperial Russian government, which at that time held Bessarabia and also claimed the nearby lower Danubian region, wanted a share in the business, and the Turks, the official possessors of a number of Black Sea ports, also wanted theirs. Each of the powers was naturally more interested in the profits from postal concessions than those from the shipping.

At this point the British stepped in and laid a railway from Küstendje to the nearest river port on the Danube just above the huge delta. The railway was only 60 kilometres long, an insignificant distance when compared to the length of the Danube itself and the distances that Danubian shipping had to cover before reaching the outlying sea ports, but it was a key operation. Thanks to this British capital venture Danubian river barges did not have to sail out to the sea nor did they have to weave their way through the maze of river channels forming the huge muddy delta. Still another advantage was that the railway circumvented Russian-held territory and was therefore exempt from Russian control.

The trip took only two and a half hours and consignments from all Danubian countries could be reloaded in Küstendje on to seagoing vessels owned by Austrian Lloyd. The stamps bearing the letters DBSR (Danube and Black Sea Railway) were thus an issue of a private British post authorized by Turkey to handle Austrian cargo in Romania in such a way as to avoid Russian control. Naturally, only a small part of the volume of shipping bore the DBSR stamps, since the bulk of the mail was transported in sealed sacks but the DBSR issues, which rank among the world's first railway stamps, are philatelically very interesting.

Today, the French National Railways deliver mail, especially parcels, to towns and villages with a railway station and the French parcel post delivers only to communities that are not served by the railways. Private railway companies operating in Great Britain are authorized to carry mail on their routes but unlike Belgian and French railway stamps, theirs are private issues.

Telegraph Stamps

Today in most countries the telegraph service, together with the telephone and postal services, usually comes under a single department of communications. However, in the 19th century most telegraph lines were privately owned, notably in the United States, Russia and many other countries. Only when the services were taken over by the state did the question arise of how to account for the fees and as a result telegraph stamps were introduced to be pasted on telegraph forms. The first telegraph service stamp was issued in 1864 by Prussia and stamps of this type were used in the Netherlands, Portugal and other countries as late as in the period after the First World War. Interesting cases of telegraph stamps are known from Spain and Chile where the post office did not have the necessary amount of letter stamps. Collectors should note that telegraph stamps cancelled by postmarks are sold for higher prices on the market than those cancelled by a stroke of a pen or by a rubber stamp.

Telephone Stamps

These stamps entitled the bearer to make telephone calls from post office pay telephones. Austria introduced such stamps in 1880 and they remained in use until 1900, while France used them during 1885—1906. Moreover, Belgium and some other countries had telephone stamps for a time. Telephone stamps usually resembled regular postage stamps in design.

Submarine Stamps

Only two countries have ever attempted to carry mail by submarine and both issued special stamps for the carriers. The first was the German Empire. During the First World War the British naval blockade in the Atlantic made the supply of certain materials to Germany extremely difficult and Germany therefore built two especially large U-boats, *Deutschland* and *Bremen*, that were to operate on Atlantic routes regardless of the surface blockade. The United States was still neutral and it seemed that the two submarines would be able to shuttle undisturbed between Europe and America for a long time. Apart from cargo, mail had to be also taken aboard to prevent it from being captured by the enemy. This was the reason why the Berlin Insurance Bank decided to establish a regular route which was to be served by the two submarines.

In 1916 special, large, high-denomination stamps were issued that bore only the name of the company and therefore constituted private issues. Envelopes with these stamps were to contain another cover with the destination address on the American continent. The commander of the submarine was to hand the letters to the shipping agent in the port of call who was to open the outer covers, take the envelopes out, put U.S. stamps on them and submit them to the U.S. Mails for further handling. Unfortunately, the *Bremen* was heavily damaged on her maiden voyage and when the United States entered the war in 1917 the service had to be discontinued.

The second case dates from 1938 and took place in Spain. Spanish Republican forces, hard pressed by the troops of the insurgent General Franco, were gradually losing control of large areas of the country and some Catalonian towns could not communicate by overland routes any more, while sea routes were constantly endangered by Franco's ships patrolling the coastal waters. The Republican government desperately needed. an operable route, and thus two small submarines based in a Mediterranean port were used as carriers. The Spanish Republican post issued a special set of stamps, but the submarine route did not remain in operation for long since the Republican regime fell soon afterwards and the idea had to be abandoned.

The most recent issue of submarine stamps had its origin once again in Germany, this time just before the end of the Second World War. A large German army group operating in

Poland was cut off from the High Command and the supply bases at home by the rapid advance of Soviet troops. Since the group's naval forces included a submarine, the group command decided to use it for the conveyance of mail to those parts of Germany that had not been yet taken by the advancing Allies. The vessel naturally could not take all the mail aboard and therefore a part of the regular field post issue was overprinted with a special surcharge. After the war the stamps came to be known as the Hela-U-Boat issue. A study of historical records has revealed, however, that the Hela Peninsula was taken so quickly by Soviet forces that the submarine post was never actually put into operation. In spite of this the stamps became quite popular in Germany and fetched very good prices. In fact, the demand was so great that some forgeries even appeared.

Official Stamps

Departments of government and state institutions are almost everywhere exempt from postal charges since the payment of postage would involve complicated interdepartmental transfers of budget money. In order to designate which institutions are exempt or which articles sent through the mail are subject to postage to be paid by the addressee, most post offices either used to issue, or still do issue official stamps that are distributed among approved agencies and services. The official stamps either have a special design of their own which is not repeated on regular postage stamps, or else the latter are overprinted in the official language of the country with surcharges like *Service* (France), *Dienst* (Germany), or *Official* or *OHMS* (On Her Majesty's Service). The first official stamp was issued in 1886 in what was then British India. The British Post Office issued different stamps for the individual government departments and so did Argentina, while Württemberg distinguished between stamps for state and those for municipal authorities. Switzerland issued surcharged postage stamps for the League of Nations and its world-wide agencies based in that country.

Stamps for official use issued in Spain in 1854 had no face value but bore the designation of the weight for which they were valid. The stamps actually served as a mere check that the sending agency was entitled to postage-free mail. Today the practice is still continued in Portugal.

Military Stamps

Like the civil service, the armed forces are also exempt from postal charges. Military mail is generally required to bear the unit handstamp or one quoting the number of the statute that exempts the armed services. Furthermore, in some countries army personnel are entitled to pay lower letter rates, even in peacetime. One such country is Sweden where special stamps for the army have been issued, or France where ordinary postage stamps surcharged with the letters FM *(franchise militaire)* are used. The stamps are distributed either directly in the barracks or sold in canteens and at tobacconists located in the neighbourhood.

These peacetime military stamps must not be confused with the field post stamps issued in wartime and distributed in limited numbers among frontline trops in order to reduce the amount of soldiers' mail to manageable proportions. For example, during the Second World War Germany issued several kinds of field post stamps, at first for surface mail only, but later also for airmail and for parcel post.

Newspaper Stamps

As standards of living improved, more and more newspapers and magazines were sent through the mail every day. As newspaper companies themselves grew larger and became regular customers of the post office, the postal authorities granted them reduced (newspaper or second class) rates and issued special newspaper stamps in various denominations to be used as postage for single copies or for bundles of various sizes.

The world's first newspaper stamp was issued by Austria in 1851. One of the best-known stamps of this kind, bearing the image of Hermes, is another old Austrian issue. This latter stamp had no denomination but was printed in different colours for single copies and for small and large bundles. Its classical design, featuring the mythological messenger of the Greek gods, has been forged several times and some of the cases involving forged issues have become notorious even outside Austria.

Another popular newspaper stamp is the U.S. 1865 issue. Its size, 50 × 92 mm, made it for a long time the largest stamp in the world.

In time railways carrying parcel post realized that if they cut their newspaper rates they would be able to attract more business their way and some railways, notably in the United States, Belgium, Latvia and elsewhere, issued special stamps for newspaper bundles.

Postage Due Stamps

These are very common stamps that are affixed to mail by the post office itself to indicate that the recipient must pay the amount represented by the face value of the stamp, because the sender has either not covered the postage fully or not at all. For the collection of postage due ordinary postage stamps overprinted and sometimes merely handstamped with a surcharge are frequently used. This type could also include the so-called Late Fee Stamps issued by the British colony of Victoria, Australia, in 1855 and used to collect extra fees for forwarding letters posted after the post office was shut, or stamps issued by Ceylon (now Sri Lanka) and bearing the words *Postal Commission*. These stamps were used for fines imposed for default in payments of postal bills.

Fiscals

Fiscals have already disappeared from postal practice. They were issued for the payment of non-postal services like sealing letters, filling in forms or legibly addressing envelopes. Such stamps were issued by Bulgaria, for example. In Italy fiscals were used to collect fees for permission to receive mail for one's neighbours or for any other person stated in the form, and Italian post offices also used them to validate or authenticate certain documents. Somewhat unusual and completely non-postal in character were fiscals of extremely high value issued by Kenya and Uganda in 1922 for the payment of permits to hunt big game including elephants.

Delivery Stamps

These stamps were introduced as prepayment for the service of delivery into the addressee's own hands. Combined with ordinary postage stamps, they were used in 1935 in the Dominican

Republic on letters addressed to the president and the members of the cabinet. Czechoslovak 1937 and 1946 delivery issues were triangular in shape and although they remained in use for short periods only, the public quickly nicknamed them 'love letter stamps'.

Registered Mail Stamps

Registered mail stamps were used for postage on articles that were guaranteed delivery because the sender was issued a receipt and the recipient had to countersign a copy. Some registered mail stamps had a blang space on the face to be marked in ink with the registration number of the consignment. Good examples of such stamps are Colombian and Panamanian issues of the late 1880s and the early 1890s. The first registered stamp was issued by Victoria, Australia, in 1854. Besides surface stamps there used to be also registered airmail stamps. The letter R on registered mail stamps stands for the French word *Recommandé*. Registered mail stamps have already been discontinued and universally replaced by registered mail labels known as 'R' labels.

Money Order Stamps

Special money order stamps were in use in the Netherlands in 1884—1889, in Spain after 1915 and in El Salvador in 1895—1905. At present ordinary postage stamps are used everywhere on money orders.

C. O. D. Stamps

These stamps were designed for use in cases in which the sender of articles by post authorized the postal authorities to collect certain sums from the addressee. If the addressee refused to accept the article and to pay the sum due, the post office registered the fact on a special form.

Express (Special Delivery) Stamps

These stamps covered the payment of extra rates for a quick delivery. The first express stamp appeared in the United States in 1885 and depicted a running postman. There used also to be express airmail stamps, although the last part of the delivery naturally had to be covered on foot. At present express stamps have been universally replaced by dark red labels bearing the appropriate wording.

Certified (Insured) Stamps

These stamps were not issued by insurance companies as their name might imply but by postal authorities to cover extra rates levied for the insurance of valuable articles sent by post. An example of such stamp is a 1939 Mexican issue.

Acknowledgement-of-Receipt Stamps

These stamps fall only rarely into the hands of a collector. They were used by postal authorities to notify the sender, who had requested and paid for the service, that his letter had been delivered. Such stamps were used by Montenegro in 1902, while Chile issued a stamp bearing the words *Avis de réception* in 1894 and three years later another issue with the words *Avis de paiement*.

Phonopost Stamps

Strange as it may seem, the idea of sending recorded messages originated more than fifty years ago. Special rates and special stamps were devised for such 'phonoletters'. An example may be the 1939 Argentinian issue. According to the regulations of the Universal Postal Union, mail of this type has been prepaid by ordinary postage stamps since 1971.

Valuable Mail Stamps

These were designed for letters containing money or other valuables. A historical example of such a stamp is the 1865 Colombian issue.

Parcel Post Stamps

These stamps were issued by the post office rather than by the railways for the payment of parcel post carried by the mails regardless of the carrier used.

Savings Stamps

Savings stamps were used for the registration of small savings. Stamps of this kind to be used by the post office were issued in Spain in 1916 and again in 1927. Similar stamps were introduced in 1918 for Soviet Russia.

Court of Law Stamps

Such stamps were issued in 1898 by the Austrian postal authorities and remained in use for ten years in Eastern Galicia. Their function was to cover postage for the despatch of legal documents submitted to the parties in civil law cases. Similar stamps with the same function were used within the territories of Tsarist Russia, where they were issued in 1909.

Consular Stamps

Consular stamps were issued by various governments for consular use, e.g. for passports and visas. When ordinary or special postage stamps became scarce, consular stamps were sometimes used to cover ordinary letter postage. The best known examples are Russian consular stamps used by the Soviet embassy in Berlin to cover postage for letters dispatched to Russia via a special air route from Berlin to Moscow. The old Imperial consular issue was surcharged by the Soviet authorities for the purpose. A similar case concerning consular fiscals used for postage is known from Ecuador in 1949.

Sunday Stamps

In an effort to limit the volume of mail to be delivered on Sundays, when most postmen went off duty, the Belgian post introduced special stamps in 1893 that had a small detachable label or tab at the bottom. The label bore a notice *Not to be delivered on Sundays*, in French and Flemish. If the sender detached the label, the article had to be delivered, even on a Sunday. The stamps remained valid till 1914.

A somewhat different approach was tried by the Bulgarian postal authorities whose Sunday and holiday delivery stamps were surtaxed and the extra receipts earmarked to fund a sanatorium for postal employees. The issue remained in use during 1925—1950.

Return Stamps

Return stamps were issued by Bavaria in 1865 and Württemberg followed suit four years later. They were to be used by postal authorities to frank and seal those letters that had been opened by the post office to establish the identity of the sender if the article could not be delivered to the addressee.

Franco and Porto Stamps: Postage Prepaid and Postage Paid on Delivery Stamps

These stamps originated early in the second half of the 19th century — the 'classical' era of stamp collecting. According to a custom of the period the sender did not have to pay for the carriage of his mail if he did not wish to. In fact, postage was quite commonly paid by the recipient, and a number of authorities therefore used two kinds of postage stamps of the same face value. If the postage was paid by the sender, the letter bore the so-called *Franco* stamp and the addressee was exempt from any payment. If, however, for some reason or other, the sender decided not to pay the postage, the post office affixed a *Porto* stamp to the letter and the postage was collected from the addressee. The *Porto* stamp was of the same denomination as the *Franco* stamp but had a different colour.

In fact the old *Porto* stamps had a somewhat similar function to the modern postage-due stamps, although the latter are used as a penalty and the amount they represent is double the ordinary postage. This is why the current postage-due stamps are designated as *Portomarke* in German catalogues, although their function is not the same as that of the classical *Porto* stamps. Similarly, most postage stamps today represent what once used to be *Franco* stamps.

Automobile Stamps

Automobile stamps were issued when the traditional horse-drawn delivery wagons were replaced by motor vehicles — much quicker and more versatile carriers. To give the customers a choice of carrier, the Swiss post issued special automobile mail stamps in 1937 and Finland did the same in 1949. In 1919 Bavaria had issued official stamps valid for its state motor vehicle transport company. This issue was actually made from part of a postage stamp issue surcharged with the text *Freistaat Bayern* (Free State of Bavaria) that was perforated with the capital letters LK for the purpose.

Floating Safe Stamps

The name of this somewhat adventurously sounding service is familiar to those collectors who specialize in stamps of the Netherlands. These unusual stamps were used for postage of mail carried by vessels sailing to the Dutch East Indies. Mail bearing these stamps was locked in a fireproof safe standing on the deck. The safe was guaranteed to withstand temperatures up to 1700 °C and a pressure of ten kilograms per square centimetre but was expected to remain afloat should the ship sink. The stamps were issued in 1921 with 37.5 % of the receipts going to the Dutch Post Office and 62.5 % to the Floating Safe Company. The issue was necessitated by the fact that during the early years after the First World War many shipping lanes remained mined. It was finally discontinued in 1923.

Maritime Mail Stamps

Whereas state and private airlines that carry mail operate on the basis of fixed charges for various distances, seagoing vessels that took mail aboard in the past had no such rates. Agreements between the local postal authorities and shipping agents were usually of a general character only and were not based on the number of articles carried and their individual weight. In 1875, for example, and again in 1882, Mexico issued maritime mail stamps that earned the postal authorities money to be paid to English and French ships willing to carry mail when they sailed.

Although the famous first issues of Mauritius covered postage for delivery on foot on the island, they were recognized also by the captains of French ships that called at Mauritius for fresh water. In fact the most expensive letter cover in the world bears two Mauritian stamps and was sent from the island to Bombay in India. It is also a well known fact that whereas most Mauritius 'Post Office' issues have been found in Bordeaux, from where Mauritians ordered their favourite wines, not a single specimen has been unearthed in Great Britain although the island was a British colony and stamps bearing the portrait of Queen Victoria were introduced there by the British governor. The reason is quite simple: the stamps were not recognized by British captains, or rather by the British authorities in London, who were only slowly preparing stamps for the colonies at printing offices in England. Generally speaking, although ships are often depicted on postage stamps, there have been only a few special maritime mail stamps issued.

River Stamps

We have already mentioned the Austrian-controlled Danube Steamship Company that used to carry both passengers and cargo on the lower Danube. The railway network was not as dense as it is today and, since there were no good roads in the vicinity of the river, river boats were the quickest means of conveyance from Central Europe to the Black Sea. Letterboxes were therefore provided in every Danubian port, from which mail was collected by river barges prior to sailing. Although the barges delivered mail only as far as the ports of call, leaving it with the port authorities or shipping agents, the volume of mail they handled was astounding and the company soon discovered that it needed stamps of its own. Company inspectors made sure that no letter accepted for handling went without a company stamp. The company had no postage-due stamps but could impose several kinds of fine on unpaid mail. Towards the close of its Danubian operations the company even issued stamps in currencies of the countries in whose ports mail was taken aboard company ships that sailed the Danube.

Riverboat posts using their own stamp issues also existed on other major rivers. Among the best-known, most commonly used and philatelically very interesting issues were the stamps of posts operating on the Yangtze, in China.

Ferryboat Stamps

Denmark consists of many islands and peninsulas separated by straits and channels. It is hardly surprising, then, that in 1919 the Danish Post Office issued a set of 45 stamps to be used for mail carried by ferryboats across the Lin Fjord and to the Fanø Island in the North Sea.

Caravan Stamps

These stamps originated in many parts of the world at the end of the 19th and at the beginning of the 20th centuries. For example, Russian tea traders established a postal route that connected Lake Baikal with China via Mongolia. Although the main function of the route was the transport of freight, caravans also took along mail whose carriage costs were subsidized by the Tsarist government. In 1893 France opened a regular camel route in the territory of Obock, in French Somaliland, and issued two stamps for it. Iran (then known as Persia) had a similar route in operation in 1911 —1913 that used standard issue stamps surcharged with the word *Relais*. The route was served by slow-moving horse teams that were changed at relay stations spaced about 30 miles apart.

Municipal Postage Stamps

Besides state postal services, as late as the beginning of the 20th century there existed in many cities municipal postal systems that issued their own stamps and sometimes also postal stationery. Since there were thousands of these municipal systems operating in many countries, philatelists still lack a specialized comprehensive catalogue of their issues and must refer to the catalogues of individual countries. It is also interesting to note that a number of these municipal postal systems were owned by the state, e.g. in Tbilisi (Tiflis), Georgia, and even in the capital of Russia, St Petersburg (now Leningrad). In fact the first stamp issued in the territory of Imperial Russia was that printed by the municipal post in Tbilisi.

Among the stamps of municipal posts there are also those issued by private businesses that carried mail in urban districts and sometimes even ventured beyond the city limits. Philatelically interesting are stamps issued by the Stuttgart streetcar company in 1933, which were used for the payment of postage on mail carried about the city in the company streetcars. In fact streetcars are still used in many cities to carry mail. In Amsterdam, for example, one can drop a letter in a box hanging on every streetcar and be sure that it will reach the post office within an hour, since all streetcar lines converge in the centre of the city at a terminal located in front of the main railway station and the general post office. There the boxes are emptied and loaded on to trains leaving the city or forwarded to local post offices in Amsterdam. This is a much faster method than the usual one in which vans collect mail from street corner letterboxes. Unfortunately for the philatelist, the fact that the letters are carried by streetcars is not recorded on them in any way.

Zemstvo Stamps

Tsarist Russia was for administrative purposes divided into large territorial units or regions, which in turn were subdivided into provinces. These provinces or *zemstva* were administered by self-governing bodies composed of the local landed aristocracy and gentry who often controlled large territories encompassing a number of towns and villages. The Imperial Russian Post served only major provincial centres and considered its obligations fulfilled if the article was delivered at the provincial capital, although the real address could be still several hundred miles away. Delivery throughout the province had to be carried out by the provincial post, which was run and financed by the provincial authorities, who also issued their own stamps. Since there were about 200 provinces in Russia and each issued a number of stamps during the years of its existence, the total number of issues comes to several thousands. The Imperial Post stipulated that these local issues must not be identical with, or resemble in any way its own issues; otherwise there were no restrictions on the design.

Some provincial authorities issued only stamps with basic drawings in black and clerks had to colour them by hand, while others ordered theirs printed in state printing bureaux and could often boast of issues that surpass in beauty many modern stamps. These *zemstvo* issues still await comprehensive cataloguing and remain an interesting field for philatelic study. Very popular among German collectors is the collecting of stamps of the former Wenden *zemstvo*, populated mainly by German settlers.

The *zemstva* had already stopped issuing their stamps before the First World War.

Catapult Stamps

In the 20th century the volume of transatlantic mail grew so much that large ocean liners had to have permanent sorting offices to handle the post during the voyage and prepare sacks of mail for further distribution on the American continent. This was to expedite delivery of transatlantic mail, but the post office soon discovered that its efforts were largely wasted since the mail had to wait for the port authority, police, customs and other formalities before the passengers could disembark and only then could the mail be unloaded. A catapulting device was therefore designed to launch small mail-carrying planes several hundred miles before the liner reached port. By the time the liner was boarded by the harbour pilot the mail was already in the hands of the U.S. Mails.

The device was employed mainly by German liners and by the French who were trying hard to win the Blue Ribbon for the fastest crossing of the Atlantic. The French liners used catapults to launch mail-carrying seaplanes as a special ship to shore service. The fee per letter was 10 francs and was paid with ordinary postage stamps. During one voyage, however, the ship's post office lacked the required amount of 4000 stamps of the appropriate denomination. The ship's printing office had to cope with a rush order for 4000 surcharges with the new face value and special catapult mail stamps came into being.

Zeppelin Stamps

When the famous dirigibles, constructed by the ingenious designer of lighter-than-air ships, Graf Zeppelin, ventured from Lake Constance to various distant parts of the world, the Post Office recognized an opportunity and engaged the Zeppelin Company as a mail carrier. This was in 1930—1934 and the German example was soon followed by the postal authorities of other countries whose territories the Zeppelins either crossed or landed in. The new type of carrier naturally called for new rates and, therefore, new stamps. Altogether more than 20 countries in Europe, America and Africa issued special Zeppelin stamps.

The native country of these huge dirigibles, Germany, employed an identical design for an entire stamp set. The stamps differed only in their face value and some minor details, depending on the route, e.g. to South America, to the North Pole or to the World Fair in Chicago. Very popular with collectors are letters that one of the dirigibles exchanged with the Soviet icebreaker, *Malygin*, at Guker Island in Tikhy Bay. The letters handed over by the Soviet authorities at that time were also franked with special Zeppelin stamps. For more detail on Zeppelin stamps, see the chapter dealing with entires.

Rocket Stamps

Stamps purportedly intended for postal flights powered by rocket engines have been issued by many countries of Europe, Asia and America. However, all these stamps are mere labels because they are private issues used to finance rocket trial flights. If there was an agreement with the post that mail carried by the rocket would be forwarded in the ordinary way, all articles had to be franked with regular postage stamps based on regular rates. So far the only exceptions have been Cuban rocket mail stamps dating from 1939 that were issued by the Cuban administration for the testing of rockets as postal carriers in Havana.

Pneumatic Postage Stamps

Only three years after the introduction of the world's first stamp

London was also the birthplace of another invention that was to leave its imprint on the conveyance of mail. The pneumatic post operates with a conduit or pipeline in which compressed air drives a cartridge containing a letter, message, etc. Pneumatic postal systems always operate within the limits of a town. In spite of its technical limitations a pneumatic post is capable of delivering a great quantity of mail. The first special stamps for a pneumatic post were issued in Italy in 1913, and Germany, too, was to issue a number of these stamps as well as pneumatic postal stationery. Today pneumatic post is used solely for special internal communications. For instance, pneumatic conduits connect telex and telegraph exchanges with delivery departments, while privately operated systems are used for in-house communications in large banks, newspaper offices and department stores.

Courier Stamps

In 1956 the authorities of the German Democratic Republic introduced special stamps bearing the abbreviation ZKD which stood for *Zentraler Kurierdienst* (Central Courier Service). This provided postal services between various state authorities, agencies and large industrial enterprises. Several ZKD stamps were issued and, since there were various combinations of letters and numerals designating a large number of routes, a complete ZKD issue collection shows a considerable range of variations. In 1965 after the national frontiers had been guaranteed the ZKD service was discontinued and all surplus stamps were sold on the philatelic market.

Postmasters' Stamps

The name denotes stamps distributed by local postmasters for their particular neighbourhoods in U.S. cities before the introduction of issues valid for the entire United States. These stamps were issued during 1845—1947 and there were so many cities that it would be impossible to name them all here. The price of these postmasters' issues increased over the years from the nominal value of 5 or 10 cents to many thousands of dollars and some stamps of this kind are even considered unique rarities. The reason for such high prices is not an error in the printing, as in the case of many other rarities, but because so few have been found.

Missionary Stamps

In fact these stamps are nothing but the ordinary postage stamps of Hawaii. In September 1851 the official government gazette published a decree which prescribed the postage of five cents for a letter and two cents for a newspaper. The legislation had to be introduced in practice by a Mr Whitney, a businessman, who also acted as postmaster at Honolulu. His stamps were entirely typeset, i.e. not only the text and the numeral denoting the face value, but also the ornamental framework. It may well be asked what these stamps have in common with missionaries. In fact, the name 'missionary stamps' dates from a later period and was coined by philatelists, since the largest users of these stamps had been missionaries active on the Hawaiian Islands. All stamps of this type discovered later were found on missionaries' letters.

It is interesting to note that one of these stamps, an unused two cent blue, remained the most expensive stamp in the world for some time and that missionary stamps used to be even more popular that the first issues of Mauritius. The unique, unused two cent blue changed hands several times and has been associated with many fascinating stories and legends. A murder is even said to have been committed for possession of the stamp.

Camp Stamps

These stamps were not regular issues but were distributed by the inmates of prisoner of war camps and concentration camps. Letters prepaid with these stamps were naturally barred from postal systems outside and were delivered only within the camps. Printing blocks were usually hand-carved from bits of leather or rubber. One of the best-known issues of this type were stamps printed in the Allied prisoner of war camp in Woldenberg, Poland.

Stamps that were printed in concentration camps originated under somewhat different circumstances. For example, those from the camp in Łódź, Poland, were made with the direct approval and even assistance of the Gestapo who confiscated the entire issue, probably with a view to selling it later on the market for its rarity value. Since camp stamps were always unofficial issues printed on any paper and with any ink available at the time it is extremely difficult to say which specimens really originated in the camps and which are later speculative forgeries. In a collection, camp stamps, cancellations and stationery may serve only as period documents illustrating conditions during the war.

War Propaganda Stamps

These stamps, or rather forgeries, are also known by philatelists as 'espionage forgeries', although they were never used by secret agents or in intelligence operations. Among the best-known examples of this type of issue are stamps produced during wartime in Great Britain that caricatured the stamps of Nazi Germany, for example a German stamp commemorating the first Nazis who died for the cause and depicting a young flag bearer and a text ... *Und ihr habt doch gesiegt* ... ('And yet you have won a victory'). The English retained the text and the design layout but replaced the picture of the flag bearer with the portrait of General von Witzleben executed as one of the ringleaders in the plot to assassinate Hitler. The forgery entirely subverted the message of the Nazi stamp although at the first glance it was almost identical to the original issue.

Another of these stamps retained the traditional Nazi design with Hitler's portrait but replaced Hitler with the head of Hans Frank, the German governor-general of occupied Poland. In this way British intelligence wanted to drive a wedge between the leading Nazis, since Hitler's paranoid mistrust of his henchmen was a matter of common knowledge.

However, the Nazi intelligence services did not remain inactive, either. German forgery workshops located in the concentration camp at Sachsenhausen produced caricatures of British stamps commemorating the wedding anniversary of the British king and queen, in which the portrait of the queen was replaced with a portrait of Stalin depicted as an ugly old Jew. The royal crowns used in the corners of the original design were replaced by Stars of David and the stamp bore the date of the Teheran Conference. The Nazis affixed these stamps to thousands of small articles addressed to residents in Britain, whose names were obtained from phone directories. The mail bearing the caricatured stamps was then placed in British mail sacks and dropped from planes at the end of German air raids on Britain to make it look as if they came from post office vans which had been hit by bombs.

Although there existed a number of war propaganda forgeries their overall effect was much less than had been expected. The intended psychological impact was negligible since, after the all-clear signal had been sounded, security forces immediately started searching the target area and mail sacks containing articles with these stamps attached were destroyed. In spite of the fact that hundreds of thousands and perhaps millions of similar forgeries were printed during the war they are only rarely to be had on the market. Stamps of this kind naturally constitute an interesting period document but essentially they are anything but philatelic material.

Since President Roosevelt was known to be an avid stamp collector, the U.S. forces headquarters in Italy had a birthday present made for the President in the form of a stamp. It copied the usual design of Nazi German stamps with the portrait of Hitler, but the lower part of the face was replaced with that of a skull signifying death. The stamp became a subject of rumours that circulated among U.S. troops all over Europe and many a G.I. wanted to get hold of a specimen to bring home as a souvenir from the war. Since the demand created a market, unscrupulous operators moved in to profit from the situation. As a result, what had been a war propaganda forgery, was

Popular pre-revolutionary Russian stamp currency; the imprint on the back certified that the stamps could also be used as small coins

forged again and specimens were sold at exorbitant prices. Collectors should be reminded that this type of issue has nothing in common with true philately.

Stamp Currency

Since they are official, monetized prints of the state, stamps are quite close in character to currency, and in fact specially altered stamps could be used to purchase merchandise in Russia in 1915 and again in 1917 when small coins were in short supply. The post office issued cardboard stamps whose face served as an ordinary postage stamp while the reverse side bore the state emblem and a note that the stamp was also valid as a coin. It was up to the holder which way he decided to use it.

Stamps with no Face Value

Many stamps of this kind have been issued all over the world. Some were either purely commemorative or charity issues, others were simply distributed free. The first such stamp appeared in Spain in 1869, and the Spanish government issued them to reward and honour the author of a book on the history of the Spanish post. The author was entitled to free postal services for life. A similar Spanish stamp appeared again in 1881, while Romania followed suit in 1934. Still later, in 1946, Romania issued free stamps for the benefit of the Red Cross. In 1924 Italy introduced stamps to finance public libraries and Spain issued free stamps for the deputies of the Cortes, the Spanish Parliament.

Fictitious Stamps

These prints actually do not deserve the name stamps at all since, although they are made to resemble them, they are mere miniature pictures. They have been issued to immortalize or popularize an author, artist, etc., or to defame or discredit another person in the eyes of the public. Such is essentially the character of a number of labels of this kind, some funny, others less so, which appeared after the establishment of the Paris Commune in 1871. Other examples of fictitious stamps are those of the 'Republic of Montmartre', produced by artists residing in the bohemian quarter of the French capital on the occasion of local festivals, in order to finance the festivities. These stamps of course have never been taken seriously.

POSTCARDS

Almost everybody must be familiar with these small cards of standard size and a light-coloured surface to facilitate writing and reading. The top right corner of the face side is imprinted with a stamp. This may be similar to the adhesive postage stamps used on letters. Sometimes, however, the design, colour or the printing process used are altogether different. The denomination of postcard stamps is usually half the ordinary letter postage.

Postcards are also monetized postal stationery issued by postal authorities but as an invention they are almost thirty years younger than the first stamp. The actual birth date of the postcard is Oct. 1, 1869, but as the history of the stamp can be traced back earlier than the actual date of its origin, i.e. May 5, 1840, so the forerunners of the postcard considerably predate 1869.

The idea of reducing a letter with an envelope to a single piece of paper and carrying it for a fee lower than that for a closed cover probably originated in Germany. It was Heinrich von Stephan, privy councillor of the Prussian postal services, who first promoted the idea publicly. Stephan devoted his entire life to postal work and presented the novel idea at the fifth all-German postal conference held in Karlsruhe in October 1865. The conference did not reject the proposal but nor did it order it to be taken up. At the time, postal officials, and especially von Stephan himself, were faced with the problem of uniting the individual German states, principalities and cities to form the North German Postal Union. The final decision on the postcard proposal was being continually postponed until there appeared another man who adopted the idea, reformulated it, but whose main contribution was to publicize it. The idea caught on and the introduction of the postcard soon followed.

On Jan. 26, 1869, a newspaper, *Neue Freie Presse*, published an article on the advantages of postcards both for the customers and for the postal services. The author of the article was Dr Emanuel Herrmann, professor of economics at the Vienna Military Academy. His arguments impressed the general public and professional circles alike and, as a result, as early as Oct. 1 of the same year the first yellow and black postcard came into existence. Soon the popular novelty was being widely used not only throughout the Austro-Hungarian Empire but also in other countries. The first German postcard appeared in 1870, shortly before the originator of the idea, Heinrich von Stephan, became the Director-General of the North German Postal Union. The first home of the postcard, however, remained in Vienna, and visitors who come to Vienna today to see the Museum of Technology will find a room there devoted to Dr Emanuel Herrmann and his first postcard.

The postcard can be used here as an introduction to the concept of postal stationery, i.e. stationery with an imprinted postage stamp, which cannot be separated and forms a whole with the paper. Nevertheless, it is permissible in some countries to cut out uncancelled stamps from postcards and to use them for postage, or rather a part of it, on a letter. However, postcards without imprinted stamps, that is, with the stamps cut out, cease to have any philatelic value. It should be also remembered that stamp cutouts used on letters constitute philatelic curios.

Since not only the stamp but the entire postcard constitutes a postal print philatelists scrutinize, study and compare every square inch. It takes only a minor variation in the printing — not necessarily in the imprinted stamp — and philatelists will recognize a new postcard issue and study the reasons for the departure from the standard. Such variations may involve wider or narrower address lines, the frame on the address side, the order numbers that sometimes appear on postcards, etc. Moreover, just as a true philatelist studies the quality and colour of stamp paper, so does a collector investigate the paper and possibly even the size of postcards. According to international agreements the minimum dimensions of postcards today are 14×9 cm while the maximum permissible size is 14.8×10.5 cm.

At first only the back of the postcard was used for messages, while the entire front was reserved for the address. It was only as late as 1907 that the left-hand side of the front was permitted to carry the message, too. Still later, a part of the message space on the left-hand side was reserved for preprinted lines where the sender could write his address.

In time some clever person thought of joining two postcards together, one intended for the outward message (known as the outward half) and the other for the reply (the reply half). The only thing the sender had to do was to write the address. In 1971, however, the Universal Postal Union decided to discontinue reply postcards because of technical problems associated with the automatic handling of mail. Electronic equipment handling mail cannot identify the preprinted stamp on the reply half that originates in a foreign country and cannot, therefore, decide whether the card is properly marked, which means that any such card would be automatically rejected by the machine.

Postcards were marketed in some countries in booklets containing from six to ten or in sheets of five or six that made it possible to type several addresses, with only one insertion in a typewriter. This saved time, but the sheets still had to be cut into separate postcards before mailing. At the present time sheets of postcards are not used, but many countries have introduced postcard vending machines.

Most postal authorities issue postcards intended only for domestic mail and, if a postcard is mailed abroad, its preprinted stamp must be supplemented with adhesive stamps to make up the postage required. Besides standard postcards, some countries also issue special postcards to commemorate important events. Since these postcards are expected to be sent abroad, they are already imprinted with stamps of an appropriate denomination. Such commemorative issues represent interesting supplementary material both for territorial and topical collections.

At the beginning of this century, about the same time that it was agreed that the left-hand side of the postcard could also be used for the message, some postal authorities authorized various, mostly private, overprints of a commercial advertisement character. Still later the entire reverse side of postcards became used solely for advertising or promotional purposes and thus two types of postcards came into being as we know them today: those with a picture, landscape photograph, drawing or some other decoration only on the left-hand side of the face (address) side, known in German as *Bildpostkarten*, and those with pictures on the entire reverse, known as *Ansichtspostkarten* (picture postcards). Today, the overwhelming majority of greetings and wishes appear on postcards that developed from simple picture postcards. These greeting cards have been designed for all kinds of occasions, carry a printed text or slogan and the only thing that the sender has to do is to sign them. Greeting cards are especially popular in the United

States, where postcard sales constitute a major part of stationers' business.

Another type of postal stationery that has developed from postcards is cards that bear no stamp and are handled free of charge. Most of the best-known kinds originated in wartime and there are very few serious collectors who do not have in their collections one or two field postcards sent from combat zones or field hospitals. The number of these cards printed during the two world wars is staggering. Somewhat smaller issues were prisoner of war cards, printed either by the belligerent powers themselves or by the International Red Cross. All postal administrations handle prisoner of war mail free of charge.

The next best-known type of postcards that bear no imprinted stamps and require no adhesive postage stamps are official (service) postcards, usually forms like draft cards, requests to attend a medical examination, etc. that require to be filled with only a few supplementary data.

Postcards can also reveal that interesting phenomenon, so fascinating for the philatelist, known as mixed postage, in other words, stamps issued by two different authorities. Mixed postages generally occur when the stamps of a regime which has been overthrown or superseded have not yet been invalidated and stamps issued by the new regime are already in use. Mixed postages will be discussed in greater detail in the chapter on letters.

Postcards with imprinted stamps may be also surcharged, again either because of a change in the system of government, occupation of the country by a foreign power, or changes in postal rates. The original numerals denoting the face value are blackened or obliterated by several lines or bars and overprinted with the new face value, possibly also with a new currency.

Like letters, postcards may also bear various postmarks and labels denoting the carrier or service (airmail, registered mail, etc.). Generally speaking, postcards represent valuable period documents for a collection.

Postcards fall, or used to fall, in various categories:

Airmail Cards

According to universally accepted customs the edges of airmail postcards are printed in strips of two or three colours, usually representing the national colours of the issuing country. This decorative design is supplemented with a preprinted notice to the effect that the article is prepaid for airmail. The notice is in the national language and in English or French.

Automobile Postcards

These used to be issued in Switzerland for routes serviced by motor vehicles.

Pneumatic Postcards

Postcards designed for the pneumatic post were usually of a smaller size than standard postcards and were often printed on coloured paper, for example pink or pale blue, as in France, to facilitate the sorting and separation of pneumatic mail from ordinary mail. In France these cards were known as *carte-telegrammes*, perhaps because of their rapid delivery. Compared with telegraph messages transmitted by a wire service, these *carte-telegrammes* had several considerable advantages, notably that they were very cheap (the postage was a mere 30 centimes) and that the number of words was not limited. Obviously, their major disadvantage was that they were restricted to this particular type of carrier and could be delivered only within a single town or city.

Postcards can be also classified according to the issuing authority:

Postcards Issued by State Authorities

These postcards are intended for domestic and international circulation and as such they must meet the requirements of the Universal Postal Union. The imprinted stamp usually retains the size, shape and layout of adhesive postage stamps and is often of the same design. There is no firm rule, however, and in some cases the imprinted design may have irregular edges or may be split into several parts and can, in such circumstances, hardly be called a stamp. Heligoland, for example, issued in 1878 a postcard on which the designation of the country appeared separately in the centre top part of the address side and the letters were embossed as if the name were reflected in ice. The

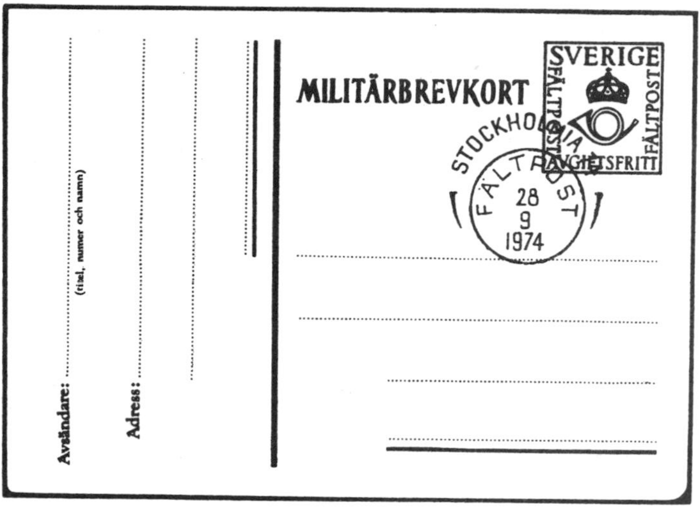
MILITÄRBREVKORT
SVERIGE
FÄLTPOST
FÄLTPOST
AVGIFTSFRITT
STOCKHOLMIA
FÄLTPOST
28
9
1974
Avsändare:
(titel, nummer och namn)
Adress:

Swedish military personnel postcard

top right-hand corner, the part that usually bears the imprinted stamp, remained empty. The national emblem was located in the top left-hand corner, under which was a separate decorative ribbon design bearing the face value.

Local Postcards

(Postcards Issued by Private Local Postal Organizations)

In Germany alone there were almost 100 of these issues. Their design was usually more conservative or traditional than that of the Heligoland postcards mentioned above and they were printed on papers of different thickness and colour. A diligent philatelist could build a very interesting collection of these local postcards, especially those that were actually handled by the post.

Zemstvo **Postcards**

Since the Russian *zemstvo* (provincial) posts were authorized to handle mail only within their jurisdiction, mail sent to other provinces and submitted at the border for further processing had to be supplemented with postage stamps issued by the Imperial Post. This practice led the Pskov *zemstvo* authorities to issue a postcard with a one kopeck *zemstvo* stamp imprinted in the top left-hand corner, while the top right-hand corner was preprinted with a frame for a three-kopeck Imperial Post stamp. There was also a note that postcard was good for delivery within the entire Russian Empire. The Imperial Post, however, felt that the postcard design represented an infringement of its own privileges. Consequently the Pskov *zemstvo* post was forced to obliterate the frame and the note with black ink and imprint the postcards with another notice to the effect that the card was valid only within the territory of the province. The Imperial Post simply disliked the idea of being an equal partner to a mere *zemstvo* authority. While the design of an envelope is the prerogative of the sender, the design of official postal stationery is not and the Imperial Post therefore rightfully refused to handle an article of an unauthorized design.

Functionally postcards can be also divided in the following way:

Advertising and Business Reply Postcards

Apart from the ordinary postcard the most common type is the business reply card. The first cards of this kind were already in existence at the end of the 19th century and have remained in use ever since, with many modifications. Business reply cards can carry advertising copy, pictures, or both. They were manufactured in two ways. The postcards bearing a printed stamp and issued by the postal authorities were subsequently printed with the advertisement. Alternatively, large companies sometimes commissioned the post office to print a stamp on cards of their own design. Some companies used these postcards for advertising and sales promotion, leaving enough free space for a message and the address, and either gave them away as gifts to their customers or sold them below face value.

Postcards with Charity Stamps

Besides ordinary postage these postcards also bore a surcharge. The receipts from the extra earnings went to various charities, services or beneficiaries stated on the card, e.g. relief for old people, widows' and orphans' funds, inhabitants of disaster areas, etc.

Ready-Printed Postcards

They are issued all over the world for periodically repeated messages. For example, in 1970 the Soviet postal authorities began marketing ready-printed postcards intended for long-distance chess matches; the postcards show a printed chess board. Although every move requires a separate postcard, these postcards have proved very popular because chess enthusiasts can play their favourite game with opponents living hundreds or thousands of miles away. Similarly, postcards with ready-printed order forms for the booking of long-distance railway reservations have been available in the U.S.S.R. since 1966. The price is included in the face value of the postcard.

There are also postcards whose ready-printed texts were needed for a limited period only, e.g. **Missing Persons Postcards** that were used after the Second World War. The address was already printed because all postcards of this type were centrally collected and delivered to missing persons bureaux. In Germany the nominal value of these postcards, which was two marks, covered the postage and the expenses for the often long and difficult search, while bureaux in other countries did not charge any fee for the search.

ENVELOPES

Stamped Envelopes

By the early 17th century the supply of paper had become abundant but letters were still formed by two sheets of paper folded and tucked one inside the other. The envelope as we know it today is of a much later origin and was invented in England in the late 18th century. In Brighton there was a stationer named Bremer who observed that ladies staying in this fashionable seaside resort were often bored and wrote a lot of correspondence but were anxious to keep their letters confidential. Being a good businessman, Bremer soon found a solution and started selling folded paper pockets of various sizes, into which a letter could be placed and sealed by means of a flap, and thus the modern envelope was born.

So-called Sardinian horses — postmarks on letter papers of the Sardinian post denoting payment of postage

From the philatelists' point of view envelopes fall into various categories. Let us ignore for a moment envelopes pasted all over with adhesive postage stamps with perfect cancellations proving that the letter has been handled postally. What interests us at the present time are envelopes that have also been handled, carry various postmarks and labels and have printed or embossed stamps, but not stamps that have been pasted on to them. Such envelopes are included in postal stationery. As in the case of postcards, philatelists are also interested in the imprinted or embossed stamp, in the size of the envelope, the quality of the paper used for its manufacture, various other printed data and, last but not least, the shape of the sealing flap on the back. When the production of envelopes ceased to be a manual affair and machines cutting identical flaps from paper sheets took over, flaps became an identification mark of issues of certain postal authorities.

It is interesting to note that the first envelopes with printed stamps are in fact much older than the Penny Black. In the early 1820s the Sardinian postal service, whose routes served the entire Mediterranean far beyond the frontiers of the Kingdom of Sardinia proper, started selling letter paper with printed postmarks featuring a tiny postal courier mounted on a galloping horse and blowing a horn. There were three different face values and the postmarks were placed on the paper in such a way as to appear next to the address when the sheet was folded. The 'Sardinian horses', as the postmarked sheets came to be called, were probably the first examples of postal stationery, although they did not look like modern envelopes.

The first envelope with a printed stamp, postal stationery in the modern sense of the word, was actually an issue of the municipal postal authority in Sydney, Australia, which introduced it in 1839, one year before Rowland Hill's reform advocating the use of adhesive postage stamps. In fact, it seems that smaller local posts showed a greater initiative as regards the issuing of postal stationery than did national governments, because the example of Sydney was soon followed by other cities. The first postal stationery that appeared on the market in Imperial Russia were envelopes with postmarks, the forerunners of adhesive postage stamps, which were originally introduced by the municipal postal authorities in St Petersburg, Moscow and other large Russian cities. The practice prevailed from 1845 till 1883 when the Imperial Postal Service issued its first envelope with a printed stamp.

One of the most interesting covers that a philatelist can obtain for his collection is the first official British prepaid postage envelope, known among stamp collectors as the Mulready envelope. William Mulready was the winner of an official competition held by the British Post Office at the same time as the competition for the first stamp design. The Mulready envelope was also issued in 1840. It does not bear a printed stamp, but a large, intricate printed design with Britannia sitting enthroned in the centre and flanked by groups of animals and human figures, often of an exotic origin, and symbolizing the extent of British rule. Like Hill's stamps, the Mulready envelopes were also printed in two colours, black (one penny) and blue (twopence). In addition, the price was printed at the bottom.

It is interesting to note that the envelope actually failed with the public and, unlike the Hill stamps that soon became very popular, the Mulready envelopes were frequently ridiculed and caricatured. The unpopularity of this first British postal stationery also explains why only a relatively few specimens have been preserved in a condition worthy of mounting and why they are so rare.

Nowadays, more and more postal authorities are marketing postal stationery decorated with colourful motifs and designs to make them more attractive. Even such conservatively minded countries as Great Britain issue envelopes with Christmas motifs, special designs promoting major stamp exhibitions, etc. During the two decades 1953—1974 the Soviet Union, where collecting postal stationery is very popular, issued a total of 9,374 different postal envelopes catering specially for topical collectors.

Among the first countries to introduce postal envelopes with printed stamps were the various German states, notably Württemberg, which kept issuing them until the Württemberg post was incorporated in the all-German postal system.

According to the agreement of the Universal Postal Union posts accept for handling only envelopes that are between 14 and 23.5 cm long and between 9 and 12 cm wide. An envelope intended for a collection should retain its original dimensions and specimens torn during opening and subsequently trimmed cease to be envelopes and constitute cut squares or cutouts that have an altogether different philatelic value to entires.

Besides regular envelopes with printed stamps intended either for local or domestic delivery postal authorities also issue:

Registered Envelopes

These appeared for the first time in 1845 and bore a printed note, *recommandé*. Territories served by the British postal system use registered envelopes with a blue cross covering the entire address side.

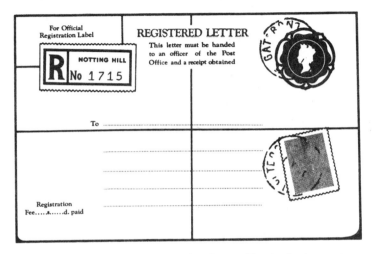

Registered letter with one imprinted and one affixed adhesive postage stamp; the characteristic cross on the envelope is used for registered mail by the British Post Office

Airmail Envelopes

These constitute one of the most common varieties of postal stationery. Their imprint details specify that they are to be carried by air and the edges are trimmed with single-colour or multicolour strips. The Soviet post has also issued registered airletter envelopes.

Privately Printed Envelopes

This is government-issued postal stationery bought wholesale by large businesses that have their own address printed either as the sender or as the addressee, for example on business reply letter envelopes. In 1961 an envelope was issued in Poland for the placing of orders with the Book and Science Publishing House. The printed stamp was in the shape of a bookshelf full of books. This was a rather special case, since postal authorities usually imprint private envelopes with regular stamps.

Official Mail Envelopes

These usually bear the imprint of the official stamp in use. The printed stamp is sometimes overprinted with the national emblem, some other symbol of the state authority or the name of the agency using the envelope. The Württemberg post, for example, is known to have issued more official than ordinary stamped envelopes.

Money Envelopes

In the past, banknotes and other valuable papers could be placed in an envelope in the presence of a postal clerk. When the envelope was delivered, its opening also had to be witnessed by a clerk who handed the money to the addressee, keeping the envelope as a receipt. Money envelopes were abolished after the introduction of money orders.

Pneumatic Post Envelopes

These used to be issued by a number of postal authorities, among them the German Reichspost, the Austrian post, etc.

Unstamped State Post Envelopes

Such envelopes did not carry a printed stamp but a note explaining why the cover was not franked, e.g. *Königliche Angelegenheit* ('Royal Matter'), *Fürstliche Angelegenheit* ('Princely Matter'), etc. because a number of royal, princely and aristocratic ruling families and other important personalities had the privilege of free postage. Envelopes of this kind were issued for ordinary mail and airmail, registered and other services, and were used not only for personal correspondence but also for that of various court institutions and offices.

LETTER CARDS

Letter cards are another kind of postal stationery issued frequently by many postal authorities. A letter card is basically a sheet of paper with gummed edges on one side. When the sheet is folded the gummed edges are glued together and the message remains confidential. To facilitate opening, the gummed edges are perforated and the letter card is opened by tearing the gummed edges off. Letter cards are also the only kind of postal stationery that differ in size depending on whether they have been used or not. The outer side of the paper sheet where the address is written bears a printed stamp of the same denomination as that used for ordinary letters.

The originator of the idea of a letter card was K. Akin of Hungary and his invention was soon adopted by many countries, including the old German states. At present some postal authorities also issue decorated or illustrated letter cards for many occasions.

According to their function letter cards can be divided into the following types:

Surface Mail Letter Cards

These are usually made from white paper although some authorities also use coloured papers.

Air Letter Forms

These are usually printed on thinner paper and have coloured strips on the edges like airmail envelopes.

Official Letter Forms

These used to be printed in certain countries for official correspondence. For example, in 1890 the Argentinian government issued six varieties of these forms for use by various ministers. All were of a uniform size, 244 × 126 mm.

Advertising Letter Forms

These were made by postal authorities on receipt of special orders from large businesses that used them for advertising purposes as gifts to their customers.

Pneumatic Post Letter Forms

Such forms used to be extremely popular because of their small size and thin paper which made it easy to insert them into the tubular cartridges used in this kind of urban postal service.

Telegraph Letter Forms

They were issued in Hungary for sending telegrams from localities with no telegraph office. The letter form with the message was delivered to the nearest telegraph office, opened and the message then transmitted by wire. The nominal price of these forms also included the charge for a five to ten word telegram.

Prepaid Answer Letter Forms

These were used until 1900 in some countries, notably Argentine and Uruguay.

Private Local Letter Forms

These were once very popular and quite common. This type of stationery was delivered to addressees living within the municipal boundaries within four to six hours after posting. Historical statistical data show that on Jan. 1, 1898, for example, the Munich Courier Service delivered some two million letter forms with the season's greetings.

AEROGRAMS AND OTHER POSTAL STATIONERY

Aerograms are airmail letters which are sent without a separate envelope. A sheet of thin paper is folded and sealed by gummed flaps to keep the message confidential. The minimum size of aerograms is 14 × 9 cm, the maximum 22 × 11 cm. Their weight must not exceed five grams. Philatelist distinguish about thirty types of aerograms, on the basis of their size, method of folding, the design of the sealing flaps and the layout of the address side with the printed stamp. Many aerograms have, in fact, specially designed printed stamps. Although they have been abolished in certain countries, some postal authorities continue to issue various kinds. There are also aerograms with colourful designs on the back.

Special Aerograms

Just as there are stamps brought out specially to mark important events, so some postal authorities issue also aerogram blanks designed to promote matters of interest. For example, Czechoslovakia issued an aerogram in 1978 to commemorate the World Philatelic Exhibition in Prague.

Official Aerograms

These are used for the same purposes as official envelopes and postcards.

Pigeongrams

Pigeon post is dealt with in the chapter on postal carriers. Modern postal services use pigeons as carriers only occasionally and purely for promotion purposes, for example, during major philatelic exhibitions or important national and international events and celebrations. In 1966 Czechoslovakia issued a pigeongram with a printed stamp. The released pigeons carrying a rolled pigeongram attached under their wings headed first for their home loft where the messages were placed in ordinary envelopes and handled in the same way as any other mail.

Newspaper Wrappers

Wrappers are strips of paper of appropriate size and carrying printed stamps, which are wrapped around rolled newspapers, magazines or other periodicals and glued together. The newspaper wrapper was introduced in 1861. Similar wrappers used to be issued also for books and other periodically mailed publications. They were issued by the larger German principalities, Austria, France and other European countries. There also existed official wrappers for the mailing of official circulars, gazettes and other items that bore official printed stamps.

Savings Cards

These are cards divided into twenty or thirty 'fields' or frames, with a stamp printed inside the first frame. This type of postal stationery is quite unique since, although it bears the emblem of the postal service and is issued by the authorities, the post does not carry it as mail but uses it to record deposits of small savings. The frames are filled with adhesive unused stamps purchased by the bearer of the card and when the card is full the owner presents it at the post office, the stamps are cancelled and the total of their nominal values is added to his credit. Savings cards used to be quite common in Austria-Hungary, Japan and Russia and are still in use in countries like Germany, Ireland and the United States.

Postal Money Orders

These can be described as postal stationery since in the early days of their existence they carried a printed stamp. Money orders were introduced in 1866 and some countries even issued official money orders and special ones for military personnel. In 1905 the Austrian Post Office issued a postal money order to be used for the payment of newspaper and magazine subscriptions.

Parcel Post Orders

These originated in the same way as money orders. It is interesting to note that the posts also used to carry parcels of bank-notes which large banking houses sent to their branches at home or abroad. The post guaranteed delivery even of such unusual articles but naturally for higher rates. For example, in Germany, even before the inflation of the 1920s, a parcel of banknotes worth several hundred thousand marks had to be covered with postage of the order of three hundred or more marks. Such a large number of postage stamps could of course never fit on a small slip and therefore extra slips had to be attached to it to accommodate the additional postage stamps. When large parcels containing notes worth several million marks were mailed, even the attached slips were too small and postal clerks had to affix the stamps to large sheets of wrapping paper, cancel them and hand the sheet over to the sender as a receipt. In fact sheets several square metres in size, all covered with stamps, were quite commonplace. Naturally, such large sheets would be somewhat impractical to mount in a collection. Moreover, they do not constitute postal stationery.

A similar situation existed in 19th-century Switzerland where coins, too, used to be mailed prior to the introduction of currency transfers and the postage for these parcels naturally depended on their weight. These two examples, however, must be distinguished from practices prevailing during periods of inflation, when even letters had to have special accompanying sheets to take all stamps required for the postage.

International Reply Coupons

International Reply Coupons are issued on watermarked bond paper by the Universal Postal Union for use by the postal author-ities of individual members. The face value of the coupon covers postage for two continental letters. When the customer buys the coupon the office postmarks it and the sender encloses the coupon with his letter. In this way he prepays the reply and the sender of the reply needs only hand in the coupon when he posts his reply. The post office cancels the coupon and keeps it as a receipt for accounting purposes. The letter itself bears no postage stamp.

Postal Labels

These adhesive stickers are not postal stationery, carry no face value and are used on mail to designate the carrier or service prepaid, the conditions of delivery or other important data. Labels, which may be replaced by rubber stamps, can be affixed either by the post office or by the customer himself. According

Express, registered and airmail labels from various countries

to an agreement of the Universal Postal Union some labels have a traditional colour regardless of the country of issue.

Pale blue labels are used for airmail. They bear the words *Airmail* or *Par Avion* and the equivalent in the national language of the country.

Bright red labels are reserved for special (express) deliveries. The text may be either in French *(Exprès)*, or in the national language of the issuing country, for example, *Special Delivery* or *Durch Eilboten.*

Dark red labels with the text *Valeur Déclarée* signify that the article contains an object of the value declared on the cover.

Yellow labels with the text *Franc de taxes et de droits* signify that the article is delivered free of postage.

To this group of postal labels belong also the familiar registered mail labels, known as 'R' stickers. Since they carry a specific value they may be affixed only by postal clerks. The registration label bearing the name of the locality and a registration number is proof that the article has been registered under that number in postal records and that it will be handed over to the sender only upon his signing a receipt slip. There are many individual philatelists as well as clubs that specialize in collecting these 'R' stickers.

Letters may also bear a number of other auxiliary labels and hand-written remarks. For example, if the addressee is unknown, the delivering post office will affix a label with the world *Inconnu* on the article or, if the letter is to be returned to sender, a *Retour* label can be used. There are many possible variations and such labels, in combination with other rubber stamps, postmarks and penmarks, provide a rich source of information for the philatelist about the way in which mail travels round the world.

CANCELLATIONS AND POSTMARKS

Postmarks have been accompanying mail for several centuries and in fact became associated with postal services much earlier than postage stamps and labels. Postmarks used to be imprinted on both the face and the reverse side of letters long before envelopes were invented. Historians consider that the oldest known postmark originated in Venice. It had a circular shape and in the centre bore the coat of arms of the Count of Milan, Francesco Alessandro Sforza, surrounded with the text *Mediolarum Cursores*, i.e. the Milanese couriers. Although these postmarks bore no date, scholarly research has pinpointed the year of the first cancellation as 1499. The oldest dated postal cancellation is 1661, although this does not necessarily mean that all postal cancellations since the late 17th century have shown the day, month and year, or possibly even the hour of posting.

As can be seen from letters in the period before stamps, which should in any case form a basis for a good collection anyway, postmarks and cancellations had undergone years of development before they came to resemble cancellations as we know

Maltese cross postmark used to obliterate the first stamps

them today. Incidentally, some cancellations used to obliterate the world's first stamps were still 'dumb'. i.e., they bore no date. These mute cancellations were in the shape of an ornamental Maltese cross.

Dumb cancellations came in various types. They were originally composed of dots, lines, small squares and geometrical patterns like grilles, wreaths, etc. In their layout they formed circles, squares or rectangles, elipses, and regular polygonal areas both delineated and nondelineated. It is simply impossible to list them all here and a collector interested in these early cancellations is best advised to consult the literature on the subject. The history of postal cancellations reveals many interesting facts because, as the political map of the world gradually changed, various postal authorities continued using the cancellations of their predecessors, although often for a different purpose. Such phenomena were quite common in the territories served by the German Reichspost, sometimes even by the earlier Prussian Post, which continued using the ancient local posting cancellations dating from the period of the Thurn-Taxis post as delivery, transit and other postmarks.

During the 18th and in the early 19th century letters usually bore postmarks denoting the place of posting, e.g. *Prag* ('Prague'), later *von Prag* ('from Prague') or *v. Prag*. The name of the place was soon supplemented with other data. The word

Franco, written in longhand or stamped by means of a rubber stamp, signified that postage had been paid on posting. The *Franco* rubber stamp was either red or blue in colour. In that part of continental Europe which had come under French influence during the Napoleonic Wars this manner of denoting prepaid postage was prescribed by postal regulations and the custom prevailed even under the Prussian Post, the only difference being that the letter 'C' was replaced with 'K'. However, since postage could also be paid by the recipient, the *Franco* cancellation had its counterpart in the so-called *Porto* cancellation. Already during the 18th century postmarks with the name of the place also carried the date.

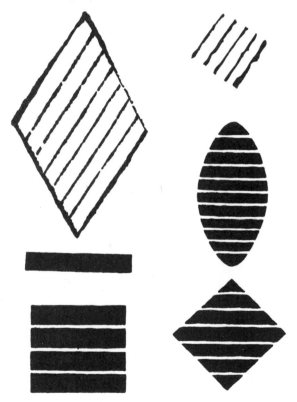

Various kinds of mute cancellations from different periods and countries

Various kinds of mute cancellations from different periods and countries

The development of postal cancellations in Britain was somewhat different. In 1680 William Dockwra and his partner, Robert Murray, leased the operation of the London post and transformed it into their famous London Penny Post. Since postage for the London post was one penny, Dockwra devised a triangular handstruck mark with the inscribed text PENNY POST PAID. Letters in the centre of the mark denoted individual city offices. Because of its excellent organization, the Dockwra operation succeeded in something no modern postal system can guarantee its customers any more, i.e. a delivery of mail to addressees living within the city limits only a few hours after posting.

On the other hand it should be remembered that 17th-century London was not as large as it is today and that the postal clerks of the period did not have to cope with millions of articles every day. Letters from this period also had another postmark, a predecessor of the later delivery (arrival) cancellations. This was a simple heart-shaped design that bore a numeral with the abbreviation *Mor.* (morning) or *Af.* (afternoon) above it. The cancellation was struck on the letter by the delivery postman.

Some 100 years later the system was adopted by several countries on the Continent, including Württemberg, which introduced circular cancellations with the delivery date and the number denoting the delivery round of the day.

While postmarks in some advanced countries revealed a number of data...

...those used in other countries did not give anything but the posting office number

Let us now go back to the posting cancellations that still provide the basic data concerning the handling of an article. This time our historical excursion will take us once again to 17th-century England, some 20 years prior to the establishment of Dockwra's Penny Post. At that time the office of Postmaster-General was held by Henry Bishop who became dismayed at the lack of organization and efficiency of postal services as well as at the lengthy delivery times and started therefore looking for a way to improve the service. On his orders the post started using small, circular postmarks 13 mm in diameter and divided in two by a line running through the centre. The upper semi-circle carried a two- or three-letter abbreviation of the month, while numerals in the lower semi-circle denoted the day. The year was not given.

The Bishop postmark represented a great step forward in the organization of postal services and the first historical cancellation of this kind discovered on a preserved letter dates from May 17, 1661. This particular cancellation confirmed a delivery two days after the letter had been posted in another city. On Bishop's orders, letters were to carry both posting and delivery cancellations. It should be also mentioned here that the Thurn-Taxis post adopted posting cancellations a century later and was followed by other European posts.

Posting cancellation of the 18th-century London Penny Post; the letter in the centre identifies the posting office

Small arrival cancellation of the Penny Post giving the time of arrival

Strangely enough, even today, when machine handling of mail calls for maximum standardization, posting cancellations are not uniform in design. It is only natural then that no standardization was possible 200 years ago.

Cancellations come in many shapes, some of which have become quite popular with philatelists because they resemble

The first modern postal cancellation; it was 13 mm in diameter and was used by Henry Bishop for his London post in the 17th century

Horseshoe cancellation, 1865

familiar objects, e.g. horseshoes, millwheels, butterflies or loaves of bread. There was even a cancellation nicknamed, quite unpoetically, the sausage cancellation because of its shape. It even appeared in two versions as a single and double sausage design.

Mill wheel cancellation used in Bavaria in the mid-19th century

Very soon, however, most cancellations were equipped with the numerical or letter code of the posting office and still later with the name of the place and the posting date. This does not mean that mute cancellations ceased to exist altogether. Mute cancellations often prove useful, especially in wartime when security is the prime concern. Many stamp collections contain covers or entires with cancellations in which placenames and even dates are obliterated. The practice was quite common during the First and Second World Wars and all the warring powers obliterated the codes denoting their official routes.

Numerical cancellation used in almost all of Europe in the second half of the 19th century

Daily cancellation

Single circle scalloped French cancellation

Field posts had cancellations with their own numerical codes. Mute cancellations can also be found on civilian correspondence dating from wartime and the period just prior to it. For example, post offices in Sudetenland, the Czechoslovak border territories ceded to Germany after the Munich Agreement of 1938, continued using old Czechoslovak cancellations with the Czech placenames removed until they were supplied new cancellations by the German Reichspost. Localities that had only a Czech name retained nameless cancellations for quite a while. A similar situation was repeated after the war when German placenames were removed from German cancellations used in liberated Czechoslovak territories. Mute cancellations can be also found on wartime military mail.

In the 19th century cancellations often bore various abbreviations. For example, in 1852 letters in France were being struck with the letters BM which stood for *Boîte mobile* (movable box), which in practice meant a mobile post office or a travelling post office located in a railway carriage.

Another well-known, early 19th-century cancellation common in France and other European countries bore the letters PP. The abbreviation stood for *Port partiel*, or partial postage, and meant that the postage paid covered only a part of the route, usually as far as the frontier, and that the rest of the postage was due. This type of cancellation was also used by the Thurn-Taxis post. To make things even more complicated, the most common meaning of the abbreviation was *Port payé*, or postage paid. The PP cancellation was used with this meaning during the pre-stamp era in France and elsewhere. However, the practice prevailed in many countries even after the introduction of postage stamps. The letters PP standing next to the stamps signified that the postage paid was found to be correct and that the article has been fully prepaid.

Although in the early days posting cancellations came in many shapes, circular shapes were gradually adopted almost everywhere. The circular cancellations were composed of one or two circles, in the latter case concentric ones. Later, the dividing horizontal bar was added to carry the data denoting posting time. Also very common were oval-shaped cancellations. Again, these were at first composed only of a single elipse, later of two concentric ones. Mute cancellations formed by the ovals or a single elipse with a thick line are still widely used by the U.S. Mails for the obliteration of large number of stamps on registered mail.

Single-elipse cancellations with the name of the posting office were quite common in the second half of the 19th century in the United States, Germany and Russia. Double oval cancellations bearing the words *Gebühr-bezahlt* were used for a long time by the German Reichspost and could be found on letters even after the Second World War. Oval-shaped posting cancellations became standard for travelling post offices and railway post offices as well as for certain kinds of packets. The route designation, consisting of the place of dispatch and destination could — and in some case still can — be seen under the top curve of the elipse. Such cancellations naturally also carry the date and usually even the number of the train. A letter that was conveyed in the mail carriage of a train and was subsequently reloaded into another train might carry several train cancellations, which enable the philatelist to reconstruct more complicated routes. In fact, using the timetable an inquisitive collector can even calculate the waiting times at various railway junctions.

Apart from the two German states, oval-shaped travelling post office cancellations are still used in Denmark. Railway post offices and the postal material processed by them are studied by many specialized collectors and clubs all over the world.

There have been, from time to time, some peculiar forms of cancellation of postage stamps. Many stamp collections contain material cancelled not only by instruments made from rubber or metal but also from all kinds of other materials. For example, the Free City of Danzig, which constituted an independent postal territory for some time between the two world wars, is known to have used only the text cancellation bearing the date. All the other stamps found on the letter were obliterated with a mute cork handstamp. In the 19th century, when Bohemia and Moravia were still a part of the Austro-Hungarian Empire, some rural offices used beautiful cancellation handstamps carved in solid wood. Since the names of these localities were predominantly German, several of these ancient wooden cancellers were used again in 1939 when Sudetenland was annexed by Germany. When the war was over, the old cancellers became useful again, this time, however, only those with Czech placenames. Such anomalies are yet another example of the provisional measures adopted during unsettled times, especially at the beginning and end of hostilities.

Postmarks have also been a cause of many outrages and scandals. In fact sometimes their use had to be strictly regulated. It is well known how modern cancellation machines, postmarking enormous quantities of mail at great speeds, can smudge postage stamps, especially if the letters are fed into the machine too quickly and the ink does not have time to set. This, however, is not a new problem and postal clerks experienced the same thing in the 19th century. It is hard to tell whether the real cause was overwork or simply malice, boredom or a combination of the two.

In the 19th century postage stamps frequently depicted sovereigns in full regalia. Kings wore bemedalled uniforms and queens their priceless jewels, but all had a dignified expression on their face in order to present their best image and one to be remembered by their people. To deface the sovereign's portrait was an insult to the head of the state — a serious felony — and, thus, the only people who could do so without fear were in fact postal clerks. Thousands of fat black cancellations daily smudged the faces of rulers in many countries of the world. Some took no offence, others simply issued royal decrees to the effect that imprints of the cancellations should be neat and legible, but there were also a few who were not content with this. For example, Isabella II, Queen of Spain, who ruled from 1833 to 1868, was very capricious and even tyrannical. She tried to prevent such a defacement of her regal head by ordering extra large cancellations with a blank centre that formed a decorative frame around her portrait on postage stamps.

Ferdinand II, King of the Two Sicilies and Naples, went even further in trying to protect his face from being smudged by the clumsy hands of anonymous postal clerks. Stamps bearing his face were permitted to be cancelled only with special handstamps featuring two laurel branches. The imprint was to be made solely below his portrait because the laurels were supposed to emphasize the king's glory rather than overshadow it. Offenders were subject to heavy penalties.

A more recent case is known from Argentina. When the Argentinian dictator, President Juan Perón, remarried, his second wife, Eva, enjoyed great personal popularity. As virtual co-ruler with her husband, Eva Perón began educational and other reforms, and concerned herself with the welfare of the poor, who thought of her as a saint. When a whole set of postage stamps with her portrait was issued Perón decreed that no cancellation must ever touch her face. Similar ordinances, both public and unofficial, have appeared in the Vatican and other countries.

The truth is that even collectors hate to see stamps defaced by excessively black, fat and smudgy cancellations. They often ask postal authorities to avoid this, by means of notes typed directly on the envelope, by means of stickers and sometimes even by means of rubber stamps announcing that the postage stamps on the letter are intended for a collection.

Somewhat marginal to the history of postal services are the cancellations of camp posts that operated in prisoner of war camps during the First and Second World Wars. The inmates manufactured these cancellers from all kinds of materials at hand, including shoe soles, bits of sheet metal and other scrap. Letters prepaid with camp stamps and decorated, rather than truly cancelled, with camp post cancellations were naturally delivered only within the compound and never reached the outside world. Collectors regard them as philatelic curios and value them as such, but in fact these cancellations are mere period documents that have little if anything in common with the regular postal services and their history.

Modern cancellations can be divided into calendar and auxiliary kinds. The latter are used to mark certain kinds of mail. Apart from the placename, calendar cancellations sometimes give also the region or the administrative unit, the numerical code of the post office, the posting or delivery date, and, in the case of larger offices in cities, also the hour. In some countries cancellations for express (special) and pneumatic post deliveries specify even the minute. The legal systems of many countries recognize the date and hour of postal cancellations as official proof that deadlines have been met, etc. Post offices using several cancellers distinguish the latter by lower-case letters located at the bottom of the cancellation. In some cases calendar cancellations even incorporate short slogans that may, for example, promote various local products, a typical industry, or some historical event associated with the place.

The sizes and shapes of calendar cancellations are not internationally standardized but most stamp-issuing countries attempt a certain uniformity in the cancellations used on their territory and try to lend them a distinct character. With only a few exceptions, most postal authorities nowadays use circular calendar cancellations. While manual cancellations have ceased showing promotional slogans, a practice that used to be extremely popular in Germany between the two world wars, machine cancellations have, especially recently, been almost always accompanied by various slogans and graphic decorations.

The so-called rolling cancellations showing the day and the minute of posting and used in large post offices in many countries are included with hand cancellations. The band or space between regularly repeated cancellation imprints is filled with symmetrical linear or dotted patterns.

Calendar cancellations are divided according to their function in postal services:

Posting Cancellations

These are in fact the very first postmarks that letters receive when adapted for handling and constitute a legal proof of this. For this reason it is extremely important that the day and the hour should be clearly legible. At the same time the posting cancellation is used to obliterate the stamp or stamps. Formerly, the posting cancellation was put on the letter next to the stamp and the latter marked with a mute cancellation.

Double circle cancellation from the early 20th century

Turkish polygonal cancellation

Rectangular cancellation for mail from a particular box, Germany, 1878

Contemporary London machine cancellation

Arrival Cancellations

These are stamped on the letter upon arrival at the final delivery office. In view of the enormous quantity of mail handled arrival cancellations are not usually used for ordinary mail because of the cost and time involved, but must be stamped on the back of registered, certified and sometimes even express (special) deliveries.

Transit Cancellations

These are used by airport and railway station post offices in sorting and junction centres. These cancellations are also stamped on the back of the envelopes. They may sometimes be made in countries that seemingly have nothing to do with the route in question. For instance, in the early days of airmail service a letter from Moscow to Prague travelled via Germany and since the Prague-bound mail left German territory in Dresden, letters airmailed from Moscow to Prague bore a Dresden transit cancellation. In cases of more complicated routes, mail may even bear several transit cancellations.

Railway and Ship Route Cancellations

Such cancellations are stamped on articles that are not carried in sealed mail sacks and are sorted *en route*. If the article is not posted directly on board the train or ship the route cancellation becomes, in fact, a transit one and as such is stamped on the back. If, however, the article is posted on board, the route cancellation is used to postmark the stamps and the imprint

Zeppelin cancellation, 1913

Zeppelin ship (onboard) cancellation, 1931

constitutes a posting cancellation. Obviously, no route cancellation can be used as an arrival postmark. Articles may of course carry more than one of these cancellations.

Commemorative Cancellations

Commemorative cancellations are sometimes issued nationwide or to all post offices in a town, but mostly they are made for a specific office only. Although commemorative cancellations may come in various shapes and sizes, they must supply all the data shown by regular cancellations. If some of this data is not shown, then the commemorative cancellation is placed next to the stamp or stamps and these must be cancelled by an ordinary calendar cancellation. Commemorative cancellations

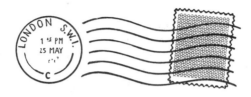

Contemporary London rolling cancellation

Contemporary English and Swiss machine cancellations

are issued for various occasions such as anniversaries, exhibitions, congresses, state visits, etc. If, for instance, an exhibition marked by a special commemorative cancellation remains open for a longer time and the cancellation gives its duration, then it cannot be used as a posting or arrival postmark.

Besides containing the officially prescribed data commemorative cancellations are often accompanied by designs, slogans or promotional texts. In some countries commemorative cancellations are sometimes struck in colours other than black. The government of the Czechoslovak Republic and later, also, of the so-called Protectorate of Bohemia and Moravia, occasionally used hand-operated cancellation machines of a special design that made a three colour imprint, for example the centre in blue, the frame in red and the text between in green.

Topical collectors take commemorative cancellations as a welcome source of acquisitions for their collections while territorialists ascribe to the cancellations a somewhat different value, since for them they constitute relevant period documents. To obtain all commemorative cancellations, even of a single country for a single year, is often rather difficult since some countries issue up to 500 such cancellations annually.

Cancellations by Favour

There are collectors who, in their effort to acquire a philatelic souvenir issued to mark some important event, will affix a stamp or a set on a sheet of paper or an envelope and ask the post office to cancel these stamps for them. Sometimes they subsequently write an address on the envelope cancelled in this manner to make it look more authentic. However, it should be borne in mind that such souvenirs are in fact nothing but fakes and an experienced collector will recognize them as such even years afterwards. These artificially produced covers have no place in a bona fide collection.

First-Day Cancellations

According to the practice of postal organizations, these cancellations can be divided in two groups. One is formed by whole First-Day Covers (FDC) issued officially by the authorities. Their cancellations are often printed by the letterpress

125

process. Good examples of this type of cancellation will be found on FDC issues of Czechoslovakia and Sweden, for instance. The second group consists of cancellations made on the first day of validity of a new stamp issue, on either official or privately prepared covers. The cancellations are carried out by special hand or machine cancellers designed solely for the occasion. In many countries these cancellations are designed by experienced graphic artists using decorations relevant to the particular topic. Letterpress cancellations are made only on envelopes that have been prestamped with the new issue and collectors cannot therefore just present themselves at a post office with their own envelope and stamps and ask for a first-day cancellation. Topical collectors are especially interested in these cancellations and use the designs to supplement or illustrate the theme of their collections. To make the design of the cancellation legible, many postal authorities have adopted the practice of printing the cancellation not only on the stamp or stamps but also next to them.

It is worth noting that first-day cancellations of the Soviet post carry a bilingual text in Russian and French.

Last-Day Cancellations

Special cancellations are used to obliterate some stamps on the last day of their validity in certain towns or post offices. For the philatelist, the first- and last-day cancellations record the period of validity of the issue in question, although last-day cancellations are not as common as first-day ones and have appeared only recently.

Field Post Cancellations

These usually show only a few data. Apart from the name of the field post they disclose only its number and the date. In some countries military posts operate even in peacetime and their cancellations do not differ substantially from those of field posts. An interesting exception to the rule are the cancellations of Army Post Offices serving the U.S. troops stationed in the Federal Republic of Germany, because they occasionally commemorate certain events.

Later Cancellations

These are used in some countries only to obliterate stamps that have been handled postally without having been marked in the usual way at the post office. If a regular calendar is used for a later cancellation, the data shown would not represent the actual time of the acceptance of the letter for handling and later cancellations must therefore be supplemented with an explanation.

Auxiliary postmarks that have been approved by the Universal Postal Convention can be divided into several groups:

Postmarks Designating Mail Class

Lettre — the French word used in international traffic to denote a letter, especially in those cases when the article does not appear to be one at first glance, for example when printed matter is accompanied by a written message and the article has been therefore accepted and prepaid as a letter.

Imprimé — printed matter. Some countries, however, are now using the designation open article (unsealed, second class mail). Since printed matter is handled at various reduced rates, a handstamp, *Imprimé à taxe réduite*, is sometimes also used.

Cécogramme — matter printed in Braille delivered either free of charge or at reduced rates.

Postmarks Designating Service

Recommandé — registered. Such postmarks will be found on contemporary mail only very rarely and if so, probably only on letters from overseas. European and major overseas countries have already generally adopted the use of 'R' labels.

Avis de réception — acknowledgement of receipt, sometimes abbreviated as 'AR'. Such articles must have an attached receipt slip that has to be signed by the addressee upon receipt and returned to the sender.

Renvoi par avion — denotes that the acknowledgement of the receipt is to be returned by airmail.

A remettre en main propre — strictly private, to be delivered into the addressee's hands only. Any alternative means of delivery is forbidden and the article cannot be merely left in a letter box or with neighbours.

Postmarks Denoting Free Carriage

Service de postes — postal service matter. The text is usually printed in the place occupied normally by postage stamps, so that there is no need to stamp the envelope.

Service de prisoniers de guerre — prisoner of war mail. According to international conventions prisoner of war mail is handled free of charge.

Service d'internés — service for interned persons.

All these auxiliary postmarks can be made either by the post office or by the sender himself.

Delivery Postmarks

For obvious reasons, the following postmarks can be made by the postal authority only; they are sometimes replaced by labels:

Retour — return to sender.

Inconnu — addressee unknown.

Refusé — refused delivery.

En voyage — addressee is travelling and has left no forwarding address.

Parti — addressee has moved without leaving a forwarding address.

Non réclamé — unclaimed. Used especially for mail delivered as *poste restante* (to be collected) or for mail bearing a stipulation of the period the post must wait for the addressee to accept or collect the delivery.

Décédé — addressee deceased.

Cachets

Cachets are devices, usually hand-stamped, that are very popular with collectors because they denote special circumstances under which the article was handled or carried, for example, Helicopter Delivery or, in the far North, Dog Team

Frei lt Uverf. No. 22.
Der Bezirks-Thierarzt

Imprinted note denoting free postage

PORT PAYÈ

(P. P.)

SAN MARINO

(Repubblica di San Marino)

Contemporary letterpress cancellation of the San Marino post

Gebühr bezahlt
beim
HPA 8028 Dresden

Letterpress cancellation for bulk printed matter mail

Postal cancellations denoting payment of postage

Delivery. The cachet can also confirm any other unusual mode of transport like camel caravan, postal glider, parachute, power boat, etc. Cachets sometimes give the starting and ending points of the irregular means of conveyance. Another quite

Besuchet das
TECHNISCHE MUSEUM
GEÖFFNET TÄGL. AUSSER MONTAG
A-1140 Wien, Mariahilferstr. 212

English and Austrian meter postages

Finnish meter postage

frequent cachet is a handstamp spelling out the reason why the delivery has not been made by the carrier or service prepaid, for example, 'Van delivery substituted for airmail delivery due to permanently bad weather conditions', etc. In this context we should also mention various wreck and disaster postmarks that are made specially as the occasion arises and about whose shape there are no general regulations.

Slogan Cancellations Made by Hand

These are usually of an instructive character. The post office may use them to ask the addressee to notify the sender of his postal delivery code (ZIP code) or to explain that late delivery has been caused by the illegibility of the address, etc. Cancellations of this type may also be a purely propaganda character. The post office as a state institution may for instance urge the voters to participate in elections, etc. In wartime, such propaganda slogan cancellations are widely used by all the participants. In order to make them more conspicuous they are printed in vivid colours.

Beginners at stamp collecting should realize that stamps do not always have to be obliterated by stamped cancellations. As late as the end of the 19th century, postal authorities practised cancellation methods that will dismay every collector who happens to come across them. Almost every collector of classic issues is familiar with those energetic strokes made in indelible pen on postage stamps. Of course, classical letters so defaced, i.e. those dating from before 1880, may be used in a collection but nobody could justify a modern stamp cancelled by pen or pencil marks. The only exception may be one of those rare cases when, for some reason, the postmaster signed the stamp. For example, the most valuable stamp today, the British Guiana One Cent Red, was initialled by the postal clerk because, according to the regulations of the period, every single stamp in the sheet that was sold over the counter had to be signed. British Guiana even issued stamps with a frame and a blank centre that had to be signed by the governor as the head of state to validate the stamp and make forgery more difficult.

According to philatelic literature the first case of signed stamps is known in the British colony of Bermuda from the mid-19th century. The area covered by the postmaster, W.B. Perot, of Hamilton, constituted of about 360 islands, some of them uninhabited and others populated by only a few families. Perhaps difficulties in communications were the reason why the inhabitants of Perot's district sent such a lot of correspondence.

The postmaster was naturally very happy and he had a letter-box installed on every island where his couriers made the deliveries and picked up the outgoing mail, including the postage left there by the customers. After some time, however, the amount of mail started growing smaller and the post office was facing bankruptcy. Postmaster Perot suspected his employees of embezzlement and he decided to take action. He cut little paper squares, stamped each one with his rubber stamp and added his signature. Although the Hill stamps had already been in use in Britain, postage stamps in the modern sense of the word were still unknown in the colonies since the preparation and printing of colonial issues took a lot of time. Perot, however, was able to introduce his measures overnight. In the morning he started selling his stamps to the colonists, the postal crisis in Bermuda was over and Bermuda's first stamps issued by the ingenious postmaster became famous.

Naturally, cases like this are liable to confuse a novice collector at first and he will need to study thoroughly the literature, the catalogues and even the scholarly works on the history of the country in which he is specializing before he can tell whether his stamp cancelled with the stroke of a pen is to be included in his collection or thrown away.

In the past other means of cancelling were also used, notably a thumbprint. Another very frequent method, used all over the world, was the perforation of the affixed stamps. This method was, for example, practised in the Free City of Danzig, where postal regulations required the clerks to precancel all stamps of the face value of one zloty and more by punching holes in them before affixing the stamps. A special punching machine was even devised to prevent re-use of stamps. The Leningrad Museum of Communications exhibits one such machine, operated by a big handle, that punched holes in stamps affixed to letters. The machine was equipped with a number of strong needles that perforated the stamp with the emblem of the post office. Its only shortcoming was that it also perforated the letter inside the envelope.

At the end of the 19th century, the Chinese Post Office cancelled postage stamps with the imprint of a copper coin soldered to a handle.

In order to make the work of post office clerks easier and to facilitate cancellations some postal authorities adopted the so-called precancellation of whole printing sheets of stamps in the printing office. Postal clerks therefore did not have to cancel each article individually, which saved time. Examples of such precancelled stamps can be found among French, Belgian, Luxemburg, Hanoverian and U.S. issues.

Meter Postage Stamps

Meter postage stamps represent the most modern and perhaps even most abundant source of philatelic material available to the collector. Meter postage stamps are marks that replace postage stamps and are printed on mail by machines known as postage meters, franking machines, frank cancellers, etc. Various businesses, manufacturing companies and institutions of all kinds daily receive and discard piles of envelopes with meter postage stamps. Why bother to collect envelopes which bear neither postage stamps nor cancellations? Many people do so, because meter postage stamps are both cancellations and proof that postage has been paid. They are modern devices created by a modern society to make things more simple, rapid and efficient. Meter postage stamps record all data that is important for the sender, the post office and the addressee. Apart from this purely postal function, they serve as an advertisement for the sender because their slogans and designs incorporate his address and indicate the nature of his business. Meter postage stamps therefore constitute an important period document.

For a long time philatelists refused to take them seriously and it was only recently that they realized that these stamps could enrich their collections with documentary material that could not be obtained by other means. This might include data concerning an aircraft manufacturer whose planes form a part of their collection, or, say, information on a large banking house that featured in the background of the historic events which their collection records by traditional philatelic means.

Although the above examples show that meter postage stamps are most helpful to topical collectors, these stamps, their development and changes in design also provide interesting material for territorial collections, because they document the character and operation of the postal services of the period.

The first franking machine was made in the United States in 1897 but frank cancellers became widely used only during the 1920s. This was after the Seventh World Congress of the Universal Postal Union held in Madrid in 1920, which approved the use of the franking machines for international postal traffic. The German Reichspost introduced the machines the same year and other authorities soon followed. According to the present international regulations all franking machines must print in red. Detailed regulations concerning the graphic design of the marks are issued by individual postal authorities and are mostly aimed at establishing a uniform design to be used nationwide, the designation of the country, the size and shape of symbols representing the amount of postage paid, the location and calendar data and, last but not least, the space allocated for the name of the user institution and its advertisement slogans.

Like postage stamps and postal cancellations, franking machines, their mark designs and texts reflect the period and its character. Following the Second World War, for example, all German texts and naturally also the name 'Protectorate of Bohemia and Moravia' had to be quickly removed from all frank cancellers used in liberated Czechoslovakia, while those used in Germany had to be rid of all Nazi propaganda and symbols. A similar situation was experienced also by Austria and other European countries. Usually it took time before the new names and currencies could be inserted in the cancellers and provisional designs could be discontinued. The philatelist's task in this area is to document all such changes chronologically, if at all possible.

The collection of meter postage stamps or franking machine imprints is complicated by the fact that there are no lists or catalogues of designs available in any country that has been using them and while there is enough collectable material to be had, the collector is moving in unmapped territory, not knowing what to expect. This, on the other hand, will make the work twice as exciting. Unless your collection specializes in meter postages, the bulk of the collection should be formed by postage stamps and other philatelic material and meter postage stamps should be used as supplementary material only.

It should also be noted that the posts sometimes use frank cancellers to make posting cancellations. The machine postage meter is set to zero and the imprints of the canceller are used to obliterate adhesive postage stamps.

NON-POSTAL MARKS AND LABELS

Apart from postal cancellations and labels discussed above, letter envelopes, postcards, picture postcards and other postal stationery may also bear other labels and cachets made by non-postal organizations and institutions. As will be seen from the list below, these marks and labels are sometimes essential for further postal handling and without them the article would have to be either refused carriage or returned to the sender. Other non-postal marks and labels made with the approval of the post may also be interesting to the philatelist who can sometimes use them to reconstruct the route the article has travelled all the way from the sender to the addressee.

Military Censorship Marks

While most constitutions in the world guarantee inviolability of letters, there are still periods in history when this basic human right is suspended because governments must make sure that no security leaks that could jeopardize the national cause occur through the citizens' mail. State authorities are allowed to open the mail and screen letters and communications sent abroad to make sure that they do not contain classified information. Similar regulations apply to mail sent to and from the front, POW camps and detention centres. Military censorship has to cope with a lot of work and specially authorized officers work in postal sorting rooms, camps and army bases and censor the men's correspondence. Opened letters must be resealed and marked that they have been censored; screened postcards must be stamped. And these stamps are precisely what philatelists are interested in.

Naturally it is quite impossible to trace the oldest military

Japanese censorship mark

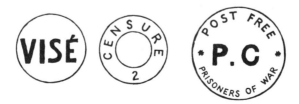

Censorship and postal rubber stamps on prisoner of war mail

censorship mark. Most probably it was merely the initials of the censoring officials. It was only later that military censorship adopted special rubber stamps without which no letter would be cleared for further handling and delivery. It is interesting to note that as late as the First World War censors' handstamps were not uniform within the individual belligerent countries. For instance, German censors used cachets with a four-line text stamped on the reverse of screened letters and signed by hand, or signature cachets giving the name and rank of the censoring officer. In fact, the censor had to use three separate cachets, an approval handstamp proper, his signature cachet and a handstamp with his name and rank in capital letters. In addition, there also existed small rectangular cachets stamped on the face of the letter, sometimes even between the address lines. Censoring duties were also performed by higher commands and to clear a letter, the censoring officer had to add his signature cachet to that of the command in question. The Austrian armed forces also employed various rubber stamps: some were composed of a single word, sometimes the censor had to sign his name next to the handstamp of the army base or field hospital command. A similar system was adopted by the Russian army. In some cases the censor used only a small circular handstamp with the name of the place where the censorship authority was located; sometimes he used larger cachets with several lines of text.

Censorship label and rubber stamps from Italy

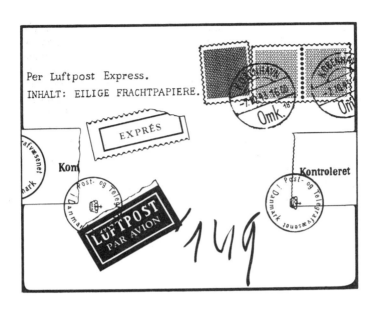

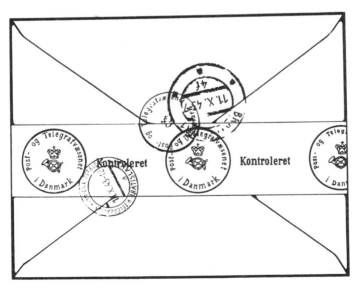

Customs tapes and marks from Denmark

Mail sent via several countries, especially that dispatched to the enemy country, almost invariably bore a large variety of censor marks both on the front and the back of the letter, a stamp being added at each stage of the journey. Typical examples of letters stamped all over by various censors' marks are letters sent from Spain during the Civil War to France and then forwarded to the country of destination after often having travelled through many other countries.

In Germany during the Second World War letters from abroad were opened and after having been censored they were resealed by an adhesive paper tape bearing the distinguishing marks of the high command while postcards were cleared by a rolling canceller featuring the same emblem. Soviet military censorship authorities used small circular rubber stamps with the state emblem and a text underneath stating that the letter had been cleared. Censorship remained in effect in the U.S.S.R. even after the war for some time before the internal situation stabilized and the flow of repatriates stopped.

Germany was divided into four occupation zones after the Second World War, and correspondence to and from the country had to be marked by the stamp of one of the four censorship services. All four powers used adhesive paper tapes to reseal letters that were opened by a side slit. A similar method was adopted by Austrian and Czechoslovak authorities. As a rule, military censorship stamps used during the Second World War did not reveal the location of the authority nor the rank and name of the censoring officer, whose identity was numerically coded, neither were the stamps hand-signed any more as had been obligatory during the First World War. During the Second World War and shortly afterwards censorship was also practised by some non-European countries, each using its own designs. Some of these rather exotic stamps may not be easily understood and the collector must consult special philatelic literature as well as experienced collectors.

Police Censorship Marks

These are used to clear the incoming and outcoming mail of prisoners. The best-known and most sought-after are letters from German concentration camps dating from the mid-thirties to the end of the war. Police censorship marks were never standardized in Germany; mostly they were of a single word type.

Customs Marks

These handstamps come in various colours and are usually small and circular. Actually, they are rather rare on letters since they are opened by customs only if the envelope arouses the officer's suspicion. Sealing of cleared articles is similar to that used on censored mail. Customs handstamps and marks are often replaced by special stickers. Even if the inspected envelope contains no object that would cause retention of the article by customs, it still must be appropriately marked by a handstamp, sticker, etc.

Onboard Cachets

Mail carried at least part of the way by a special aeroplane, balloon, ship or rocket sometimes bears marks on the address side to show this. When mail was carried by balloon the envelope was not only marked with the name of the balloon

Aircraft (on board) cachets of various airlines

but frequently also bore a special admission stamp which had no face value itself but without which the letter would not be accepted and conveyed by balloon post. Occasionally even a handstamp with the pilot's name can be found on the envelope which was then initialled in longhand by the pilot as proof that it was indeed carried by his balloon. The most famous and philatelically valued is the admission label, sometimes ranked among special stamps, devised for mail carried by the German dirigible *Gelber Hund*. Mail bearing such admission labels or stamps still had to carry full postage. Even in modern times, when mail is carried by aircraft, there are many occasions for cachets signifying that the article has been carried by a special carrier, e.g. a plane taking the Olympic flame from Olympia, Greece, to the current venue of the Olympic Games, or an anniversary, special trade fair, etc. A special group of philatelic material prized by collectors is the so-called 'first flights'. En-

First flight cancellations

velopes from the opening flights on new routes do not have to be posted at the departure and destination points only but can also be posted from any stop-over point along the route, which greatly increases the variety of first flight documents. Some airlines order preprinted envelopes for their first flights. The envelope bears all data concerning the new route so that all auxiliary or onboard stamps and marks are in fact superfluous since an ordinary postal cancellation with the appropriate text constitutes proof that the letter has been on the flight.

Disinfection Marks and Certificates

Today correspondence is almost never required to bear a medical certificate that the letter has been in quarantine. In the past, however, such bills of health were considered very important and letters bearing marks of quarantine stations or even brown spots caused by fumigation are much valued by philatelists today.

140

Collectors' Rubber Stamps and Labels

Rapid handling of huge volumes of correspondence today is often the cause of smudgy cancellations. However, philatelists naturally prefer neat cancellations, but the only thing they can do is to ask the postal clerk wielding the canceller to obliterate their stamps neatly. They either use a handstamp of their own design with a text saying that the stamps are intended for a collection and require neat cancellation, or a label to the same effect placed on the left side of the envelope face. And since there are countless philatelists all over the world who share the same concern for their stamps, their cachets or labels exist in many languages, colours and designs.

Some countries regulated the exchange of postage stamps with collectors abroad by special ordinances supervised by the customs service or the banks, later also by philatelic agencies and centres. To denote clearly letters containing postage stamps for international exchange, collectors who took part in such an exchange were issued special licence labels to be used on their letters and had to supply their partners abroad with some to be used on their return letters. Such letters were then officially opened and inspected to confirm that the contents satisfied currency exchange regulations. Collectors who wilfully avoided such currency exchange control were subject to heavy fines. The best-known and perhaps also the most interesting are Soviet philatelic exchange authorization labels current between the two world wars.

Letters and postcards often bear labels announcing the preparation of a major philatelic exhibition of others social or sporting event. Although busy postal clerks sometimes mistake them for genuine postage stamps and cancel them, such labels do not constitute postage stamps and therefore have no place on the face side of an envelope.

FIRST-DAY COVERS AND SHEETS

First-Day Covers do not bear imprinted but only affixed stamps. FDCs, as they are familiarly termed by collectors all over the world, are usually issued by postal administrations and only in some countries by large philatelic agencies or businesses. In either case collectors must buy their FDCs with the stamps already affixed and cancelled as if the covers were truly handled by the post. The cancellation date is frequently supplemented by an appropriate text that certifies that the stamps were used on a cover on the day of their validation, i.e. on the day of their official issue.

Since postage stamps on FDCs reach the collector already cancelled without having fulfilled their function in postal traffic, many postal administrations have issued directives permitting the use of FDCs for postal purposes for a period of several days and sometimes even for up to three months following the validation date as shown on the cancellation. In such cases the post does not use any other calendar cancellation showing the actual date of posting.

Since many sets contain too many stamps to fit on a single cover with enough space to spare for the cancellations and the address, two or even three covers may be issued for a single stamp set. On the other hand, if only a single stamp is issued or if the sum of the face values of an entire stamp set does not cover postage for an international letter, post offices as an exception to the rule permit necessary extra stamps to be affixed on the back and even stamps of a different issue to be used. However, the stamps affixed on the back are cancelled with an ordinary calendar cancellation showing the actual posting date rather than with the special first-day cancellation.

The issuing organizations, be they postal administrations or business enterprises, have the left part of their FDC's face decorated with designs related to the topic of the issue. In many cases these designs constitute exquisite miniature works of art on their own and are printed by sophisticated processes. Czechoslovakia, for example, usually employs multicolour steel engravings and her FDCs resemble lithographs in character; on the other hand the German Democratic Republic decorates her FDCs with colourless embossing.

When FDCs are marketed by postal administrations as speculative issues intended largely for collectors, philatelists do not value them so much. Very often an ordinary letter bearing the same stamps and actually handled by the post in the usual way carries a much greater weight in a collection than an elaborate FDC. FDCs actually resemble cancellations by favour (Fr. *par complaisance*) in character as well as letters 'manufactured' by philatelic businesses and known in German as *mache*. An orthodox territorial collector collects primarily postal documents, i.e. proofs of when and how the article in question was handled postally. Most FDCs, on the contrary, reach the collector without ever having been handled by the post since they can be simply purchased ready-made, so to speak. Experienced collectors therefore seek those FDCs that can be proved to have been used as ordinary letters. The best proof in this case is not the address but rather a registered or express label, etc., in addition to a calendar cancellation stamped on the back. Such covers have 'paid their dues' and represent genuine philatelic material worthy of being mounted in a collection.

Some postal authorities, trying to come up with a novelty, also started issuing first-day sheets. Like FDCs, first-day sheets have their stamp(s) neatly cancelled with a special cancellation device. In order to make the cancellation as neat as possible, some administrations use letterpress blocks to imprint the cancellation. First-day sheets have a certain advantage over FDCs because they do not require any space for the address and the sheet can carry all data on the new stamp, i.e. the reason for the issue, the person or event commemorated, the names of the artist and engraver, the printing process used and other valuable information. And since not every collector is always willing or able to find out about the person or event represented by the stamp, he can buy a first-day sheet with a brief outline of the vital data. Such sheets, as issued for example by the Netherlands and the Federal Republic of Germany, cannot be postmarked as proof of having been handled and some philatelists therefore make separate collections of first-day sheets that serve as a sort of birth register of their stamps. Similarly, some collectors use special FDC albums.

An interesting method of announcing a new issue was once used by the U.S. Mail. The new issue was accompanied by a letter from the Postmaster General giving information about the stamps. The stamps themselves were affixed to the letter which was then folded in such a way as to prevent the stamps from being damaged, and then placed in an envelope so that it could be mailed as a truly interesting postal document.

ESSAY

The word *essay* comes from the French and means an initial tentative effort, a trial. An essay in the philatelic sense of the word is either a design of a new stamp made by an artist commissioned by the postal autorities or else it is an entry in a contest.

Various countries have different regulations concerning these draft stamp designs. While all designs entered in a contest remain the property of the postal authorities and must not be distributed or imitated by philatelists, in some countries the rejected designs remain the property of the artist who is free to dispose of them as he sees fit.

However, it is not only the postal authorities that are opposed to the distribution of stamp imitations and forgeries. The same concern is shared by philatelists who consider as philatelically valuable essays only those prints made by entrants in the contest, or preferably those prints that the artist submitted to the authorities for approval. The artist in this sense means not only the author of the design but also the engraver. All other essays executed by unauthorized persons are viewed as forgeries regardless of the technique or process actually employed; this applies even to rejected entries that are not protected by the law as state issues.

Sometimes genuine essays are extremely difficult to distinguish from these forgeries. To be able to do so the collector would have to know a lot about the printing process and the paper used in the period when the essay in question was made, the size and colours of genuine essay prints, etc.

Essay prices are governed by the laws of supply and demand. Essay can be used only for illustration in collections. Classical stamp countries with a considerable number of stamp essays were the Kingdom of Bavaria (until 1871), the early German Empire and also to a certain extent Germany after the First World War.

CARTES MAXIMUM

Cartes maximum represent a rather distinct philatelic sub-group found only rarely in territorial collections. Although their use in topical collections is somewhat wider, *cartes maximum* basically constitute separate collections for which independent classes and groups have been established recently even at major international philatelic exhibitions. In many countries collecting of *cartes maximum* is known as *analogophilia*.

Cartes maximum are merely picture postcards that have on the picture side a postage stamp representing the same subject as the picture itself or featuring at least a major detail of the latter. The greater the analogy, the more valuable the material.

An ideal *carte maximum* would be a picture postcard bearing a postage stamp representing the identical subject viewed from the same angle. The third component is the cancellation which unites the picture and the stamp in a whole and must be also relevant to the subject. For example, it can commemorate an anniversary of the depicted event, or its slogan can promote an exhibition of flowers shown on the picture and the stamp, or it can be from the place shown, etc. The picture, the stamp and the cancellation should coincide as much as possible. What may seem a mere childish pastime at first sight can bring even an experienced collector a lot of excitement. Although the hobby of making up and collecting *cartes maximum* is more recent than territorial collecting, it has still been practised for several decades. Interesting associations of the picture postcard, the stamp and the cancellation are known even from early 20th century philatelic exhibitions, e.g. a picture of the Sphinx and the pyramids accompanied by an Egyptian postage stamp also depicting the Sphinx and a Cairo cancellation dated May 25, 1909.

In some countries collectors of *cartes maximum* are organized in specialized clubs that even publish their own periodicals. Collectors also exchange their doublets internationally. Stamp catalogues, however, do not list any prices for *cartes maximum* and any price should be based on the value of the cancelled stamp and the extent of the analogy achieved.

ENTIRES

Entires are envelopes and other covers, ordinary and picture postcards, postal slips, aerograms, and other postal articles which have been used and which have on them postage stamps, postal and non-postal labels or imprinted cancellations. Entires therefore reveal not only all the possible facts concerning the postage stamp proper but also all postmarks and other devices that have been discussed above in the chapter dealing with postal stationery. Entires are actually a treasure-trove of interesting information for the philatelist, be he a territorialist or a topical collector. Here the basic rule of all philatelic collecting must be stated: each entire, each envelope or postcard must be carefully inspected before the stamp is cut out to be separated from the backing in lukewarm water. Untold thousands of rare letters, indeed truly historical documents have been irreparably damaged just because someone tore the stamps off. How many letters from remote corners of the globe, how many messages sent home from foreign battlefields, what rich treasuries from ancient business correspondence files have ended as a pile of ashes just because someone removed stamps from them, often of the lowest face values that fetch only meagre prices on the market today if sold separately from their original cover. How many old envelopes and postcards have been found good enough only for the fire? The best example of the fact that cancelled separate stamps have a much lower philatelic value than the same stamps still attached to whole covers, or at least cut squares bearing whole cancellation and possibly also other postmarks, are the most sought-after stamps in the world today, the 1847 Post Office Mauritius issue. In the 1960s two of these red stamps with a face value of a penny each were sold in an auction at Robson Lowe for the average price of £ 8,250 each. Two identical stamps on a letter (incidentally the most expensive letter in the world) were auctioned at Harmer's for U.S. $ 380,000 in 1968, making them much more valuable than separate specimens. This perhaps best highlights the mistake that Mrs Borchard, a wine merchant's widow, made when she removed the two specimens from an old business letter and sold them separately as singles.

Naturally, Mauritian issues rank as philatelic gems and as such they are treated quite differently from mere run-of-the mill stamps that every collector has an abundance of. It would of course be erroneous to say that every stamp still affixed to a letter is many times more valuable than the same cancelled stamp removed from the cover. The example above, however, gives an idea of the situation. Although the price difference between separate specimens of other stamps and those affixed to a cover may not be so very big, the number of stamps so valued is surprisingly high. There are even cases when separate used stamps are marketable only as packet values, i.e. in packets of one hundred clean washed and carefully selected specimens with neat cancellations that do not prevent a close study, while the same stamp on a letter fetches a very good price indeed. A layman may ask why there is such a difference in price. The answer is simple: supply and demand. Some stamps are so common that no philatelist takes notice of them — although there should not be a single philatelist like this worth the name. However, when the stamps are invalidated after some time and disappear from circulation, it is suddenly discovered that entires with these stamps used to be so numerous and commonplace that they were simply destroyed and that a preserved entire with what was once a basic and common issue has become a rarity. And if the entire bears a special or commemorative cancellation, or if the calendar date represents some memorable day, the price of such an entire increases many times over. The price difference can be so high that some general catalogues have followed the example of auction catalogues and introduced prices quoted for 'on entires' besides those for unused and used specimens. Naturally, prices for 'on entires' are listed mostly for classical or special issues, surcharged stamps overprinted for extraordinary occasions like special flights, etc.

Many collectors like to display preserved entires in their collections, exhibiting the same stamp in mint condition, as used stamps, with a tab attached, as a gutter specimen, a coil version, as a block of four, etc., and finally on an entire dating from the period of the validity of the issue.

Here we should mention several peculiarities that can be found neither on postal stationery nor on separate stamps but that give many an entire a special philatelic value worthy of a collector's interest.

It cannot be stressed enough that a careful collector must be extremely careful about the 'health' of the stamps intended for his collection. Not a single perforation tooth should be damaged, much less missing. Even a damaged specimen of a rare classical stamp should be regarded as second rate and whenever possible should be replaced by a specimen in perfect condition. And a stamp that is torn, no matter how minutely, has no place in a good collection and should be immediately rejected; the same goes for specimens missing a corner or even a part of the field.

Yet there are exceptions to the rule if certain conditions are satisfied. There are stamps that have deliberately been cut in half (bisects) and these are valued very highly.

At the very beginning of this century, to be more precise on January 27, 1901, the entire German Reich celebrated the forty-second birthday of Kaiser Wilhelm II. The festivities were not limited to German territory, however, but were held wherever the German ensign flew. Vessels of the German Navy dispersed all over the globe were also ordered to participate in the celebrations in a manner that would impress the population of the countries of their temporary anchorage. The cruiser *Vineta* was then lying at anchor in New Orleans. On January 27 the crew were granted shore-leave while the commander held a deck party for the local high society. The aim of the celebration was achieved and the Emperor's birthday became the talk of the town.

Some time later, when the cruiser visited Trinidad to take on supplies, the ship's crew received a lot of correspondence that had been awaiting them. From their New Orleans acquaintances many seamen received newspapers describing the festivities in vivid detail. The sailors were naturally happy to have such souvenirs of their call at New Orleans and wanted to send them home to Germany to their families and friends. And thus the ship's bursar, who officially doubled as post office agent was soon flooded with mail that caused him a great headache.

The problem was that the mail of German Navy seamen was accepted by the Reichspost as inland mail if posted on board and carried home by a German vessel and submitted to the German post for further handling. Printed matter rates in Germany were three pfennig and that was precisely the trouble. Nobody really expected ordinary soldiers and seamen to mail printed matter home and the stock of three pfennig, stamps in the ship post office was rather low. And now suddenly every deckhand wanted to mail several newspapers, each to a different address.

The bursar was at a loss what to do and even the usually omnipotent commander could not do much to solve the problem. And thus the only post office agent on board had to help himself as best as he could. He simply took a pair of scissors and his stock of five pfennig stamps, cut the stamps into halves, surcharged each half with an overprint denoting a three pfennig value and used the surcharged bisects for postage. When the cruiser met the first home-bound German merchantman, the postmaster handed over the sack with the ship's mail and thought no more of the matter. Philatelists will be interested to learn, however, that when the cruiser returned to its home port the postmaster was held responsible although he had accounted for all the five pfennig stamps that he had sold as six pfennig ones, which incidentally did not even exist at that time.

The authorities considered his act as a violation of the strict codes of the Reichspost. The story about the unhappy postmaster's provisional stamps became known among philatelic circles and collectors quickly started hunting for bisects bearing the *Vineta* cancellation. To be more precise, what the collectors were after were not just the separate stamps but the whole wrappers (or at least cut-squares with all cancellations preserved and legible). Today, these entire fetch several thousand German marks on the market, a sum that represents an astronomical price increase as compared to the face value of three pfennig.

Let us add that the *Vineta* postmaster was not the only person in history to have violated official postal regulations. The postmaster of the Caroline Islands, then a German colony, also got himself in trouble with his superiors. A typhoon that swept the islands blew away many wooden houses including the post office building on Panope, the largest of the islands, and the postmaster was forced to cut his stamps in halves, cancel them with his official canceller and then use them for postage. A makeshift surcharge stamp spelling *Postage — 1 cent — paid* was also used after a typhoon disaster by the postmaster in Foochow, China, who had to bisect his two-cent stamps. In 1851 the Austrian postmaster in Topolčany, then a part of Upper Hungary, had to cut three kreutzer stamps into thirds and to affix narrow one kreutzer strips on wedding announcements to make sure that they arrived in time. A wedding is always a rather pressing matter and the postmaster simply could not wait for his head office to send a sufficient stock of the required one kreutzer issue.

In fact, bisected stamps, sometimes cut along a diagonal to form two triangles, sometimes along the vertical in two oblongs, can be seen quite often on old Austrian mail. If such bisects are removed from the wrapper or envelope they lose their philatelic value and become worthless. Bisect stamps are valued only on entires.

Perhaps every philatelist knows about the Saxonian Three: a brick red, rectangular imperforate issue from 1850 featuring a big numeral 3 in the centre denoting the face value of three pfennig. It is the first Saxonian stamp and to own one is the dream of every collector who is even slightly familiar with old German issues. By the 1890s philately had already become a widely popular hobby but classical issues were still relatively easy to come by and even an average collector could have them in his collection. At the same time nobody really knew how much of the stock was still available and therefore no one realized that a particular strip of five Saxonian Threes on a letter envelope was already the last specimen of its kind in the world. Even the owner of the strip, an army major named von Freund, was unaware of this and he gave it without a second thought to his son, a student at a Berlin *Gymnasium* (grammar school).

His son was also a collector but, as is often the case with young people, was more interested in attractive colourful contemporary issues rather than in classics and he therefore tried to swap the letter bearing the strip of five identical unseparated stamps with one of his classmates. However, none of his friends were interested. A class had already started but the student sat and contemplated the letter, thinking that he perhaps might be more successful if he washed the stamps off the envelope and separated the strip into individual specimens. His teacher, who had noticed that the boy was preoccupied with something he was holding under his desk, was a strict disciplinarian and confiscated the letter that was distracting the student.

The school regulations stipulated that confiscated items were to be returned only at the end of the school year but the student did not get his envelope back because he graduated and after a graduation party the class of young men were dispersed far and wide. Some obeyed the traditional German code of honour and enlisted in the Imperial armed forces, and soon forgot such childish trifles as postage stamps but the old teacher did not. When he was clearing out his desk on the day of his retirement he found among other things the confiscated letter with an attached slip of paper with the student's name on it. The teacher searched the school records and found his former student's address, put the letter with the strip of five brick red stamps in a large official envelope and posted it. To his sorrow the envelope was returned to him after some time, covered with numerous postmarks that revealed that his former student had died in battle somewhere in Africa. The rest of the story is quite prosaic. The teacher went to see Herr Glasswald, a well-known stamp dealer, the envelope with five Saxonian Threes changed hands for a tidy sum and was deposited as a unique rarity in the Reichspost Museum, a place where five single Threes would never have been displayed.

A strip of five unseparated stamps is always philatelically

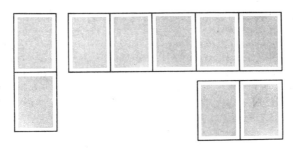

Examples of two and five subject stamp strips

Four times one may amount to more than four in philately

valuable, even if the stamps are modern. In the case of classic stamps, even a pair is highly valued. There are also letters bearing a number of identical singles; even such entires are attractive for the collector. Single specimens removed from the cover may have a minimum value but a group of such stamps on an entire has often a much higher price which is calculated on the base of various bonuses that can be found in major catalogues. A multiple use of an identical stamp to cover postage of a letter is usually a mark of uneasy times when postal tariffs do not remain stable for long, of a scarcity of higher face value issues, of inflation, monetary reforms and upheavals in political and governmental systems.

When territories change hands, period entires reveal yet another philatelically fascinating phenomenon: mail with postage stamps of two and even three different issuing countries and yet handled postally. Such mixed postages were for example quite commonplace during the *Anschluss*, i.e. annexation of Austria by Nazi Germany in 1938. Austrian issues had not been yet invalidated and therefore could be normally used while Germany had taken control of the country both military as well as postally but had not yet supplied the post with German stamps; postal clerks were thus forced to recognize

151

mail prepaid with both or with mixed postage. Naturally it did not take long for the Reichspost to supply German stamps throughout the country. The same situation in fact existed for some time in all territories occupied by Germany in the early years of the Second World War. Shortly after Hitler established the so-called Protectorate of Bohemia and Moravia in the historic Czech provinces that had been a part of the independent Czechoslovak state, letters often bore three different postages. While old Czechoslovak stamps still remained valid for some time, there were also new Protectorate issues and the post also recognized stamps of the German Reichspost although the latter were in fact used illegally since they had not been expressly authorized either by the Protectorate or the Reichspost.

Mixed postages are known from many parts of the world. Not all former colonies have new issues available on the day when they become independent. Even to surcharge old colonial issues takes time and thus letters posted in these countries often carry colonial issues, surcharged colonial issues or even new issues of the freshly independent state side by side. Any collector specializing in a territory where such changes took place is best advised to study contemporary postal regulations. In some cases the successor state declares all stamps of the old system void as of the day of declaration of independence and requires that postage be paid in a different manner, e.g. in cash at the post office and the payment confirmed by a postmark. This is done not only to prevent unauthorized use of old invalidated issues but also to prevent patriotically minded postmasters, and sometimes also sharp operators who are intent on profiting from their product, from using all kinds of unauthorized provisionals printed hastily in local printing establishments.

Whether it is because the postal personnel is delighted to see an issue of the new regime or whether it is simply ignorance of the regulations, clerks often accept, cancel and handle such stamps. If a letter bearing an illegal issue has been regularly handled by the post, its inclusion in a collection is justified to a certain extent. In most cases, however, these illegal issues end up on the market after some time, in mint condition and large quantities. Such 'stamps' have no place in a bona fide collection; the only exception may be entires that have undoubtedly been handled postally.

An example from Czechoslovak history illustrates this point. Already prior to the proclamation of the reborn republic, the

Czechoslovak governmant in exile had had stamps printed in London and Moscow to have them distributed after the war. During a short interim period until the distribution had been completed, postage was to be paid in cash. But in spite of the meticulously planned transition a whole number of provisional local issues appeared and a small number of letters bearing such stamps was actually handled by the post. Years later unscrupulous dealers offered these illegal issues to uniformed philatelists.

These provisional locals, which are valuable only if found on postally handled entires, are closely associated with another type of illegal usage, i.e. that of genuine but already demonetized stamps. Since most countries issue a great many different stamps each year postal clerks, who are usually pressed for time trying to process huge volumes of mail, sometimes do not realize that a stamp on a letter passing through their hands has already been invalidated and will accept it. In fact letters prepaid with postage stamps demonetized for years are relatively frequent. If the stamp in question is removed from the cover, it may get lost among other regularly cancelled stamps or the cancellation may be poorly legible. However, if it appears on an entire, the proof of such illegal use accompanied by an appropriate commentary will indeed enrich any collection. Sometimes it also happens that overworked postal clerks accept mail 'prepaid' with various labels. Again, such usage must be documented only on entires.

Last but not least, only an entire may be used to document overpayment of postage. Such letters often appear in collections. The reason is that fervent philatelists, usually stamp dealers, sometimes affix an entire new stamp set on a letter regardless of the fact that a mere half of the sum represented by the stamps would be enough to cover the required postage. Then they have the letter carefully cancelled at a post office and often even withdraw it from further handling to prevent its being damaged in the mail. Naturally, such bogus letters can hardly be called genuine postal documents because even if they are normally handled, they smack of a business trick. Such covers should not be included in an album of a serious collector.

Entires, or more specifically, letters, reveal yet another interesting phenomenon although novice philatelists may consider it to be too remote from everyday philately: seals.

As late as the 14th century letters were merely folded sheets of paper tied with a string and sealed with a wafer. This sealing system had one great advantage: it required no heat or flame and moistened wafers could be impressed with the insignia of the dispatching nobleman, office or city. Naturally, seals did not have a purely decorative function but prevented the letter from being tampered with by unauthorized persons. Violation of letters was still commonplace as late as the 18th century and many a high postal or governmental official owed his position to his ability to open other people's mail without leaving traces.

The situation was somewhat improved by the invention of a French merchant named Rousseau. Rousseau had squandered his wealth in India, returning home virtually penniless, but he had an enterprising spirit and soon started manufacturing sealing wax. His venture was so successful that he rapidly expanded his originally very modest business. Sealing wax was a type of merchandise that everybody needed. Envelopes with official communications were sealed by large official seals while burghers and merchants marked the wax with their signet (seal) rings. If the dry wafer seals of the past had been fragile, the sealing wax used now was still not completely unbreakable, especially when the sealed letter was handled excessively. Besides, it was not always at hand and required heat to become plastic and so people started looking for something

Registered airmail letter from Cook Islands with a characteristic cross on the envelope typical for registered mail in British and Commonwealth postal services

that would have the same sealing ability but not the disadvantages of sealing wax.

A solution was soon found in the form of adhesive paper stickers designed to resemble the heavy wax seal and also coloured red. The edge was even made irregular to make the paper seals look more like authentic wax seals and emblems and coats of arm were embossed on the paper. Since then untold millions of adhesive paper seals have been used throughout the world although the classic wax seal has not disappeared altogether. Even today some postal administrations require valuable letters to be sealed with five wax seals. In the past it was sufficient if the sender applied the four corner seals himself while the fifth was made by the post office. Today, valuable letters can be sealed only at the office with an official seal in the presence of the sender.

WORLD CLASSICS

All letters, postage stamps and other postal stationery issued or handled prior to 1870 constitute philatelic classics. If we disregard letters of the pre-stamp era, we will find that classic postages span a mere thirty years, and philatelically meagre years at that. In the 19th century it was simply beyond the technical capacities of any country to issue fifty or more different stamps every year as often happens nowadays. Most classic issues remained valid for a number of years and if they bore the image of the ruler, they remained in use as long as the sovereign lived. Great Britain, the homeland of the postage stamp, saw years during these three decades when not a single new stamp was issued. The entire issue of the former Kingdom of Saxony, for example, is limited to 19 stamps. You may rightfully ask whether 19 stamps are enough to make a collection; after all, they could be all mounted on a single album sheet.

The question, however, would be justified only from a novice collector. In the 1960s, philatelic exhibitions displayed collections of old Saxonian issues on 600 album sheets. Selection committees of major stamp exhibitions rarely accept such large exhibits. Actually, the exhibitor had originally displayed his material on 20,000 sheets. Yes, you have read the figure correctly, 20,000 album sheets, and this is neither a joke nor a hoax. The collection in question had been the result of many years of painstaking work and documented those 19 Saxonian issues with all their errors, flaws, varieties of print, paper and inks, and including all kinds of entires with cancellations documenting routes of the Royal Saxonian post, the border crossing points, various carriers employed, services provided, two and three stamp strips as well as letters with no stamps at all, mail of the royal court as well as campaign (field post) mail. Briefly, the exhibit was a perfectly documented running commentary on the operation of the Saxonian post during three or four mid-19th century decades.

At about the same time visitors to major international exhibitions could admire an exhibit dealing solely with the world's first two stamps, the Penny Black and Twopenny Blue. The creator of the collection never attempted to obtain a letter from the date of the validation of the stamps and thought it impossible to find a cover that would have used the first stamp even prior to the official date of issue. Having carefully studied all the available literature on the subject, stamps displayed at various exhibitions as well as a great number of specimens that he had gathered throughout the years, he tried to reconstruct several printing plates for each of the two denominations. Plating, as this type of philatelic study and documentation is termed, involves long hours of scrutinizing closely every minute dot and line on every specimen at hand in order to be able to tell which had come from which plate. All in all, the exhibit's creator succeeded in plating some seventeen plates, although not all of them completely. The work took him several decades to finish and cost him a lot of money.

There have been similar study exhibits dealing with the classic issues of Mauritius and documenting not only the world-famous Post Office Pink and Blue issues but also later ones including the erroneous spelling of *pence* as *penoe*.

Collecting postal stationery is less costly. Even today the first Austrian postcard issues can be had relatively cheaply and a search for postcards with the oldest cancellation can be a thrilling philatelic adventure for any collector. Such ventures naturally require a thorough study of the oldest finds so far. Incidentally, the oldest-dated postcard discovered so far has been unearthed in the 1970s outside Austria. As we have said before, there may be a collector somewhere who will discover an even older specimen.

The purpose of this chapter is also to delineate the dividing line separating world classic stamps and issues of a more recent provenance and to emphasize that even contemporary collectors can devote their time to classic issues, and that there really is no reason to envy your grandfather who considered today's rare classics modern issues.

The word classic, however, applies also to issues other than those mentioned above. Not all stamp countries had been established by the 1870s and yet their first issues constitute a group that could be rightfully designated as national classics. Many countries introduced postage stamps as late as the end of the 19th century and even after the First World War new states emerged in Europe and elsewhere that immediately started issuing their own postage stamps and rushed to join the world postal system. The period after the First World War also saw the rise of civil aeronautics, the emergence of the first airmail stamps and airmail entires. Therefore we can talk of airmail classics regardless of the fact that in the mid-19th century even the greatest visionaries did not dream of things like aeroplanes. Nevertheless, some seventy or more years have already passed since the emergence of the first airmail stamps and it therefore seems that they have already earned the venerable title of classics.

STAMP TALK

Pre-Stamp Era Letters

The very heading of this chapter implies that what we are going to talk about now are letters that originated before the introduction of postage stamps. However, since every country introduced postage stamps at a different time, it is impossible to speak of any definite period(s). Besides, large stamp-issuing countries sometimes disintegrated and the successor states issued stamps of their own. Take Yugoslavia, for example. All mail sent from the territory of what is now Yugoslavia prior to the appearance of the first Yugoslav issue cannot be said to constitute pre-stamp era letters since before Yugoslavia emerged as an independent country, its provinces had been served by Serbian, Montenegrin, Austrian or Turkish posts using their own stamps.

Generally speaking, however, pre-stamp era letters are a highlight of any collection and the older they are, the higher their value. Such documents permit the collector to trace the development of postmarks and penmarks as well as methods of sealing mail. To establish precisely the date of the origin of one's document, one must often study thoroughly not only the address part but also the message of the letter. Sometimes the date of origin can be better pinpointed on the basis of the postmark shape. Still it should be remembered that all pre-stamp era postal documents require a thorough study of philatelic and even scholarly historical literature.

Royal and Ducal Letters

Kings, dukes and other noblemen were entitled to certain postal privileges in some countries and they retained some of them even until the modern period. The most common and also the longest surviving was that of free postage. Noble houses that ruled various, sometimes even very small territories gave permission for postal routes to cross their territory in exchange for the privilege of free postage. They were also handsomely paid for such licenses. In time, as postal services were gradually taken over by the state, many such privileges were abolished but some state-operated posts continued carrying letters free of charge for certain noble houses until the First World War. Naturally, letters carried free of charge had to be marked appropriately. The bottom left-hand corner of the face side bore a handstamp, sometimes only a penmarked note *Königliche* or *Fürstliche Angelegenheit* (i.e. Royal or Ducal Matter). The back of letters of minor noble houses also bore the name and rank of the sender. Royal mail usually carried the seal of the Steward or Controller of the Royal Household. The higher the rank of the privileged person, the greater the body of people who actually used the privilege, so that even letters from contractors and suppliers could often boast of the mark Royal Matter. It would be altogether erroneous to think that letters with such a proud mark actually contained personal communications from the monarch or that they played an important role in the history of the country. Historic decrees, orders and other important documents were dispatched by special couriers while letters entrusted to the post and its various services and carriers concerned mostly everyday matters about the functioning of the royal household. In some countries these postal privileges were granted also to high church officials, especially if they held large estates. The privileges, however, went with the rank or office rather than with the person and so the practice often survived even in republican regimes. Catalogues do not list or price such letters and their value depends on the supply and demand and of course, also on how close was the sender to the titled person, etc.

Disinfected Mail

Outbreaks of cholera were frequent and widespread in the 19th century. Although some cities were never visited by this plague, the dreaded disease nevertheless left its mark on the whole world. It found its victims in Paris and Moscow alike, in London and the Riviera, in Algiers as well as Madagascar and in the densely populated areas in Asia. Hundreds of large cities were deserted by their panic-stricken populations whenever there was an outbreak and the death toll everywhere went into thousands. Physicians soon noticed that the invisible enemy did not travel through the air by itself but that it arrived by carriage or ship together with people or cargo. One of the dangerous carriers was also the mail and health authorities therefore-ordered the postal services to establish huge quarantine and disinfection stations in major ports and national capitals. In order to prevent the disease from spreading throughout the country, border crossings were also established where the incoming mail was subjected to disinfection.

The most frequently used disinfectant was simply vinegar. Small wooden boxes were fitted with wire grills and loaded with mail from the contaminated areas using a pair of long

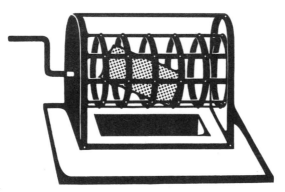

Grille for disinfection of letters by hot air, 19th century

tongs. Under the grill there was a pan with vinegar heated from the bottom by another pan containing burning charcoal sprinkled with a mixture of sulphur, sltpetre and bran. The box was then closed and holes in the bottom provided air needed for combustion. Mail was not only fumigated externally either: letters were pierced with combs studded with thick nails or the envelopes were partially slit to allow the fumes to penetrate inside. After a short but precisely determined period the mail was considered disinfected and the appropriate health authority marked the envelopes with a rubber stamp that cleared the mail for further handling.

The health services providing the fumigation were known under various names and came under various authorities. Their methods of disinfection also varied considerably. For example, Paris military hospitals in the early 20th century disinfected mail by air heated to 130 °C (266 °F). In Venice the fumigation was performed by the naval health authority; in Bavaria it was the Royal Bavarian Veterinary Quarantine Management located at Gottendorf; its beautiful rubber stamps and seals almost look like decorations. Since quarantined patients also wanted to communicate with the outside world, many inland hospitals were authorized and sometimes even directly ordered to decontaminate the patients' outgoing mail and to confirm the disinfection by a rubber stamp.

Modern medicine and drugs have checked such cholera epidemics and the postal services long ago eased the strict regulations concerning the exchange of correspondence with the stricken areas. However, these old regulations make very interesting reading today. For example, they stipulated the minimum number of steps that two postmen had to stay apart when they were handing over the mail sack, or what signals had to be used to signify that the mail had been already placed in the fumigator, or what procedures were to be adopted when the number of fumigated articles did not tally with the list, etc. Any collector who decides to study these old regulations will be fascinated to find what kind of treatment a letter had to be subjected to before it could be delivered.

Maritime and Ship Letters

It is of course not known who first dispatched a letter by ship but historical records reveal that the ancient Romans, who were mainly a land-loving people and excelled as roadbuilders, had also a naval postal authority headed by a prefect. In their time, the Ancient Greeks operated the longest postal sea route of the period, connecting Greek settlements in the Crimea and on the Black Sea and the Sea of Marmara with the Mediterranean and even up the Nile with Ethiopia.

Collections of medieval overseas letters can be sometimes seen displayed in honour classes of major international exhibitions. With Columbus' discovery of America, Europe saw a great rise in overseas shipping and soon the first naval postal routes were established. However, period postal documents are very scarce and will be only rarely found in private collections.

Modern postal services still depend on river and seagoing ships to carry mail and specimens of packet mail can be obtained by any collector. Nevertheless, mail carried by ships must be systemized as to the carrier type used.

Tin Can Mail

Tin Can Mail (sometimes also termed Canister Mail) was always a very rare service and in fact no longer exists, although several thousand letters carried by this somewhat outlandish type of service are in collections all over the world. The letters date from the Franco-German War of 1870—1871. When Paris was besieged by German troops and totally surrounded, 55 spherical zinc containers 25 cm in diameter were made and each was filled with some 500—600 letters. The containers, which had metal fins, were hermetically sealed and dropped in the Seine to float down-river. Records show that only two canisters reached the destination within the expected time while some 40 more were fished out of the river a century later, in 1970.

Between 1903 and 1946 a tin can post operated in the Tonga group in the Pacific. Since large seagoing vessels could not land at the island of Niuafoo because of coral reefs, incoming mail was sealed in tins and dropped overboard to be picked up by canoeists or swimmers.

Ferryboat Posts

Ferryboat posts still exist in many countries. The ferry in this case is no flat-bottomed barge taking people across a stream

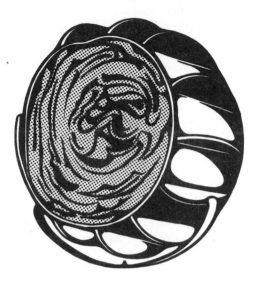

Aluminium containers used during the Siege of Paris, 1870, and fished from the Seine

but a large seagoing vessel capable of carrying a number of motorcars, railway carriages and hundreds of passengers. Ferries operate across channels, straits and other relatively narrow waters, e.g. between Dover and Calais. Major routes are served by several large ferries every day and mail posted on board is stamped by the carrier and submitted for further handling upon arrival.

Lake Posts

These can be found all over the globe. The most famous is the Lake Constance Postal Service. Since the lake shores belong to several countries, its waters are crisscrossed by several routes and it is up to the collector to choose which one he would like to handle his letter. All mail posted on board these mailboats is stamped with the ship cancellation regardless of the subsequent service.

River Posts

These have existed for centuries on all continents. The major European rivers that are used for postal service are the Danube and the Rhine. In Asia it is the Yangtze, in South America the Amazon. The Soviet post operates river services on many rivers and canals forming a huge inland waterway system. The Nile, the largest African river, has been used as a postal route for many centuries.

Mail Packets

Mail packets are rapid mailboats that usually transport mail in sealed sacks and have no post office on board that would handle, sort and cancel mail. Of course, even here certain exceptions to the rule can be found, for example the Austrian-operated Danubian post of the late 19th and early 20th centuries. On this route letters could be posted on board until sailing time. Mail packets of course operate mostly on maritime routes.

Posted on Board (Pacquebot)

Mail is also carried by ships that have their own post office on board and can therefore accept mail while on the high seas. The first country to establish such a service was Austria-Hungary which enjoyed access to the Adriatic in the 19th century and therefore operated a fleet of merchantmen and passenger liners that had post offices on board, especially those plying the transatlantic routes. Germany soon followed suit and established ship post offices on overseas routes from Hamburg

Paquebot cancellation (posted on board on high seas)

and Bremen. American, British, Italian and French liners provided similar services. Russia operated a huge company called ROPIT which was based in the Black Sea port of Odessa and its 60 vessels serviced not only the Black Sea and Mediterranean ports but went as far as China and Japan. Besides delivering mail, the ROPIT Company also issued its own stamps. It is interesting to note that while the ROPIT company issued the total of 131 different stamps, the Imperial Postal Service until the fall of the Tsarist regime in 1917 managed to issue only 87. Soviet vessels, even those plying domestic routes like that between Batumi and Odessa, also operate post offices on board.

Very popular among collectors are postmarks of the enterprising transatlantic lines of Germany. Some German liners even used small catapult-launched planes to expedite delivery in the port of destination. Huge volumes of mail were also carried by British and Dutch liners. According to international agreements every ship enjoys the territoriality rights of the country of its flag while on the high seas and can therefore operate a post office on board and sell the stamps of its country. However, when it enters the territorial waters of another country the operation of the office and sales of stamps must cease in recognition of the sovereignty of the country of call. Accepted mail is then handed over to its postal service which will not postmark foreign stamps but will mark the mail with its own rubber stamp and a label, or a rubber stamp and a hand-written pen-mark PACQUEBOT (POSTED ON BOARD). If the stamp has not been already cancelled while on the high seas, the cancellation is done at a post office in the home country.

Civilian maritime post must be distinguished from the naval post. Postal offices on board naval vessels were established somewhat later than on civilian craft. For instance, the German Navy introduced post offices on board its vessels in 1895. These German-operated posts had a special feature: cancellations were not assigned permanently to a vessel but changed according to transport and destinations. During the Second World War correspondence from ships of the German Navy was handled as field post mail.

Other German ship letters that we should consider are mail with stamps bearing the word HAPAG, an abbreviation of *Hamburg/Amerika Paketfahrt Aktien Gesellschaft* whose ships sailed on regular routes from Germany to the Caribbean, Venezuela and other destinations in Central and South America.

Mark of the French naval post authority

The stamps remained in use during the period 1857—1877, i.e. until the destination countries joined the Universal Postal Union.

During the two decades following 1857, mail posted on board the ships of the French Navy bore a date stamp and a special cancellation showing a dotted rhomboid with an anchor in the centre. At that time, French overland post used similar mute cancellations, although without the anchor symbol.

Packet posts are very popular and many collectors build highly specialized collections documenting various kinds of ship letters. The material may also include port cancellations, i.e. those of land offices issued for special occasions such as ceremonial visits of large naval vessels to friendly countries. The honour is usually reciprocated by the postal service of the visiting vessel which issues a commemorative cancellation imprinted as a courtesy souvenir for those who come visiting on board while the ship is at anchor in the port of call.

Pigeon Post Letters

Pigeons are nowadays used only rarely, usually at events such as official openings of philatelic exhibitions. In the past, however, pigeons were often a very practical and effective method of carrying mail. The first historical record of this carrier dates from 43 B.C. when Mark Antony used pigeons during his siege of Mutina, Italy. Pigeons were also used for communications during Roman campaigns in Egypt and the Crusaders first met with pigeon post during their siege of Jerusalem. The best-known pigeon post in modern times dates from the Franco-German War in 1870 when Paris was besieged by German troops. 363 pigeons were dispatched from Tours to Paris, each bird havin a light metal tube attached to its leg.

Each tube contained 18 microfilms with 70,000 words. This means that every bird carried some 3,500 letters. In Paris a special office was set up where the microfilms were projected on a screen by a magic lantern, transcribed on paper and then delivered normally. Although only a few pigeons reached their destination, they brought in many thousands of letters. In 1896 a Mr. Fricker established a pigeon post in New Zealand. The route connected Auckland with Great Barrier Island — a distance of about 65 miles. Fricker even invented a special device that signalled the return of the pigeons to their home loft.

Pigeons were deployed for communications in 1915 by Austrian troops stationed in the fortress of Przemyśl in Galicia and cut off from their supply bases, and by Japanese troops during their campaign in China in the 1930s and 1940s. Even the Congolese had a pigeon post and attempted to protect the flying messengers from large predatory birds by attaching an ingeniously designed whistle to the pigeon's tail. When the pigeon was flying the air stream made the whistle generate a loud tone that drove away the predators.

Everyone has seen designs of pigeons holding a sealed letter in their beak. Naturally, pigeons can never carry regular letters in an envelope, much less in such an unwieldy manner. Pigeon posts use thin paper that is rolled and attached under the wing, to the tail or on the back of the bird. Similar paper is also used for pigeongrams, official postal stationery issued by some administrations. Pigeon post stamps are private issues and have no place in a bona fide collection. The only exceptions are the stamps of the Fricker pigeon post which was operated privately but with the express approval of the New Zealand post.

Balloon Post Letters

Since time immemorial man has wanted to fly. His dream was first made possible with the invention of the hot air balloon which was soon to be used. The first attempt took place in Denmark during the Napoleonic Wars when one of the major Danish waterways, the Great Belt (Dan. *Store Baelt)* was blockaded by the British fleet. Records from 1808 show that at least three mail-carrying balloons were launched. The Dutch also attempted to use a balloon to negotiate the English Channel and the pilot even carried a special letter from the Dutch sovereign. Since man's experience with air navigation was still very limited, air currents carried the balloon to Coblenz, Germany, rather than to the original destination.

Then in 1870 Paris found itself in danger of being taken by German troops who had besieged the city. In the opinion of the Prussian generals no living creature could penetrate the siege. However, Paris desperately needed to communicate with the hinterland lying beyond the tight ring of enemy troops.

On September 23, 1870, the balloon *Le Neptune* was launched from St. Pierre Square, piloted by one Jules Dürüof. The balloon easily flew over the astonished and perplexed enemy formations. Two days later, *La ville de Florence* ascended from Paris, this time meeting with Prussian rifle fire. The balloon cage carried 150 kg of mail, one scared passenger, who undoubtedly prayed throughout the whole journey for a quick and happy ending of his ordeal, and three caged postal pigeons. The balloon landed safely well behind the enemy lines. Other *Ballons Montés* (manned balloons) followed and when no more pilots could be found to fly out of the besieged city unmanned balloons *(Ballons Non-Montés)* were launched and left at the mercy of air currents and luck. Altogether, 39 Paris post offices launched a total of 68 balloons carrying 10,675 kg of mail, i.e. 2.5 million letters, several passengers and some 400 postal pigeons.

According to contemporary regulations, the maximum acceptable weight for a letter was 4 grammes. In order to cut down on the weight, senders were obliged not to use envelopes but to resort to the long-discontinued method of folding and sealing sheets of writing paper. The paper was often so thin that the ink printed through and made the address illegible. There were also special *par ballon monté* postcards with a large state emblem and various patriotic slogans in smaller print. Postage for these postcards was 20 centimes for continental France and Algeria and 40−80 centimes for international deliveries. Governmental and military dispatches were carried free in sealed sacks. When an unmanned balloon landed somewhere on French-held territory, the mail sacks were immediately handed over to regular postal services for onward transmission. Several craft were carried far beyond the French border. *La ville d'Orléans*, launched during the night of November 24, 1870, flew over the whole of Germany and after fifteen hours' flight landed some 60 miles from Oslo, Norway. Some balloons crashed into the sea but were sighted by fishermen who rescued the mail. Four balloons reached Belgium and three ended in the Netherlands. One flew as far as Africa where it descended and ended trapped in a tree. The last balloon mail dispatch from Paris left on January 28, 1871. The enemy captured only five craft which means that more than sixty balloons got safely through, or rather over, the blockade.

The success of the state post also inspired many private entrepreneurs who bought huge amounts of suitable silk materials and quickly started making balloons themselves. These balloons were also successfully launched and reached their destinations carrying passengers and mail at exorbitant rates. The private flights had in fact nothing in common with the postal services since they were purely profit-oriented ventures.

The balloon post during the Siege of Paris had only one limitation — whereas it was not too difficult to get from the city to the hinterland, a flight in the opposite direction was almost impossible and this is also why all letters carried by these balloons — and there are quite a few of them in private collections all over the world — were all dispatched from Paris and addressed to destinations outside the city.

Paris was not the only French city surrounded by an impenetrable siege. The large garrison in the fortress of Metz also had to establish communications with the hinterland. On the basis of a proposal by Mr. Papillon, a military surgeon, the Army Medical and Apothecary Corps in Metz made some 26 balloons 2 metres in diameter which were gradually dispatched with the total of 185,000 letters, out of which about 65,000 eventually reached their destinations. In comparison with those launched from Paris, the balloons dispatched from Metz were smaller and therefore could carry less weight. The commander of the fortress issued an order that letters must not exceed 1 gram in weight. The military authorities even issued papers 6 ×9 cm in size that were soon nicknamed *papillons* after the originator of the idea. The nickname was in fact quite apt because the word is French for butterfly.

Almost half a century later, in 1915, the Austrian fortress of Przemyśl found itself in a similar situation and the besieged garrison managed to launch 14 balloons with field postcards, much in demand on the market today.

Although the First World War saw the final victory of heavier-than-air craft over hot-air balloons, the latter have not been entirely forgotten and are still used all over the world to mark openings of major philatelic exhibitions and sporting events. There is even the traditional Gordon-Bennett Balloon Race that takes place in various places around Europe. Well-known and quite popular among philatelists are letters carried by balloons launched by the Childrens' Villages Union of West Germany and Austria. Apart from regular postage, the letters must also carry a special label sold at a price slightly higher than that of regular postage proper. The proceeds from the sales are used to finance the launching and net earnings go to the organizing charity. Instead of labels, special non-postal rubber stamps with a balloon design are also used.

Modern balloon mail usually also has a boarding (ship) cancellation and the signature of the pilot and sometimes even that of the launcher. But regardless of the number of attractive labels, rubber stamps and penmarks that may appear on the face of balloon mail matter, the most important thing that every collector must look for is a regular postal cancellation, because only the latter constitutes an official proof that the article has been postally handled. Everything else counts as private marks — and that applies also to mail sent by charities — and there is nothing that would prove that the letter has not been made up and decorated merely for business purposes. In the 1970s the world philatelic press wrote about a police inquiry in Austria where a forgery workshop had been discovered that used printing presses and a number of stolen rubber stamps to manufacture large quantities of forged balloon post artefacts.

Zeppelin Letters

Zeppelins were dirigible airships named after their German designer, Ferdinand, Graf (Count) Zeppelin. They were huge cigar-shaped structures of duraluminium stretched with cellon-impregnated cotton fabric and filled with a light gas such as hydrogen or helium. The superstructure of the last Zeppelin model housed 25 double berth rooms with a bath, a dining room, a lounge and a library. Four oil engines with a total output of 3,600 horse power permitted a cruising speed of 135 kilometres per hour (85 mph). The first private flight of the designer took place in 1909. Later a company was formed under the name DELAG *(Deutsche Luftschiffahrts Aktien Gesellschaft)* that took over the ownership and in 1912 started commercial flights carrying both passengers and cargo. In 1919 the first regular route between Friedrichshafen and Berlin was opened. Nine years later a Zeppelin dirigible made the first overseas flight. From 1928 till 1937 the company operated two airships, LZ 127 and LZ 129. The two craft made 653 flights, out of which 189 were transatlantic, and carried 49.1 metric tons of mail, 16,169 passengers and about 40 tons of commercial cargo. A flight to North America too 40—60 hours, a crossing to South America 80—90 hours.

Both dirigibles, LZ 127 *(Graf Zeppelin)* and LZ 129 *(Hindenburg)*, visited many countries in Europe and overseas. The postal authorities of the countries where the airships landed prepared a lot of mail for each subsequent leg of the trip as an attraction for curio seekers. In fact, the amount of mail was so great that many authorities issued special Zeppelin stamps. The German post did so several times, with issues designated specially for a particular flight. Since the Zeppelin mail stamps themselves were extremely popular, too, postal administrations authorized them also for other types of mail. Besides postage stamps and cancellations for individual flights issued by the German post, other postal authorities produced their own special cancellations to be used on the day of the ship's call or flight over their territory. This is why Zeppelin mail is known even from countries where the dirigibles never landed. The mail was transported in the normal way to Berlin and from there flown, say, to America. The possible combinations are so numerous that Zeppelin letter collecting has become an extremely popular speciality.

In June 1937, LZ 129 crashed during the landing manoeuvre at Lakehurst, New Jersey, and exploded. Only a small part of the mail carried on board was saved.

Because of their relatively slow speed, high operational costs, and limited landing possibilities arising from their need for special facilities and the high risk of an explosion, Zeppelins were soon superseded by aeroplanes. In Europe, German Zeppelins met competition from airships built by General Umberto Nobile of Italy. His ships *Norge* and *Italia* made a number of spectacular flights that yielded a lot of philatelically valuable material.

Today, Zeppelin letters represent a closed chapter of philately, although since the Second World War there have been attempts in the U.S.A. and West Germany to revive airships. The life of these craft was usually limited, the flights had a more or less promotional character only and postal documents from such flights would be better classified with balloon post. However, since there still exists a great amount of old Zeppelin mail among collectors, philatelists who specialize in these letters have the chance to build an attractive collection even today.

Arctic and Antarctic Letters

The history of the exploration of the northern polar regions is as long as it is fascinating. It was the 1582 expedition of the Cossack hetman, Yermak, that contributed to the fall of the powerful Siberian khanate, annexed huge territories to Russia and opened the first postal routes to communities lying far beyond the Arctic Circle. The expedition itself culminated in the dispatch of a letter to the Tsar of Russia. During the following centuries, scores and perhaps hundreds of expeditions on foot and skis, and in ships and aeroplanes tried to penetrate the hostile icy wastelands, each getting progressively closer to the North Pole. These expeditions also used various means of communication with their bases back in civilization. As important historical documents, their letters and reports, however, will be found in museums and archives rather than philatelic collections. Postal material documenting man's activities beyond the Arctic Circle that have reached the hand of philatelists are of a more recent or even contemporary origin.

Due to man's perseverance, ingenuity and courage, the Arctic regions now yield vital raw materials, and there are numerous scientific research stations working there as well as other settlements with harbours and airports. What used to be isolated outposts of civilization are now regular townships with schools, hospitals, shopping centres and post offices. In the U.S.S.R. some two hundred and forty post offices of various kinds operate beyond the Arctic Circle: some are *oblast'* (regional) distribution and sorting centres but there are also one-room offices manned by a single clerk who receives and dispatches mail and doubles as a postman, with a territory that often has no permanent roads. In such districts, postal delivery still depends on traditional, time-tested carriers. For example, on Vaygach Island in the Barents Sea, mail is still delivered by a sledge drawn by a dog team between December and May and there are even routes served exclusively by reindeer or moose teams.

The Arctic, however, is not entirely lacking in railways. The northernmost railway in the world is a spur connecting Norilsk and Dudinka on the Taymyr Peninsula in the U.S.S.R. Trains operating on this railway incorporate postal carriages where mail is sorted during the trip. Dudinka is the starting point of the route carrying mail to the post office on Dickson Island. In summertime, i.e. from July till September, mail is brought in by a small tug; in winter helicopters are used. From Dickson Island mail is delivered to a number of outlying bases of various scientific and geological expeditions. The northernmost cancellation of a permanent post office is that used by the postmaster at Cape Chelyuskin. Man has already become so accustomed to living in the Arctic that post offices in the far north can even afford the luxury of issuing special and commemorative cancellations. Arctic cities in the U.S.S.R. regularly hold winter sports games on a rotational basis and philatelists naturally demand and also obtain special cancellations for their material. Special cancellations are also used in locations where the railway crosses the Arctic Circle.

Canada has also had a long history of exploration and settlement in the north. Ellesmere Island projects so far into the Arctic Ocean that Admiral Perry selected the island as the starting point on his historic journey to the North Pole in 1909. Today, a large research station operates on the island and there is also an army installation. Incoming mail is delivered to these outposts by dog teams while outgoing letters are shipped by plane or helicopter via a U.S. military base on the north coast of Greenland. Also very interesting are Arctic postal routes operated by the Swedish and Norwegian posts in the northernmost reaches of their territories, and the Danish post in Greenland. For instance, on Spitzbergen Islands (Nor. Svalbard) there exists a whole network of postal offices serving the administrative centres and scientific research bases as well as the numerous tourists and even the mining companies. Besides Norwegian packets, mail from Spitzbergen is also taken by Soviet vessels since the U.S.S.R. operates two leased mines in the area. The Soviet mail is handled by a collecting office operated as a branch of the Murmansk head office on the Russian mainland.

By far the most fascinating and also the most popular of Arctic letters are those posted directly from North Pole stations, known throughout the world under the abbreviation SP (Rus.

Severnyi polyus, i.e. North Pole) accompanied by a numeral. So far, there have been already more than thirty stations of this kind. These scientific research bases are located on ice floes and sea currents keep them close to the Pole. The first such station (SP-1), established in 1937 had no post office and neither did the following two. The Pole was won postally only by the second tour of duty of the personnel at SP-4. A post office at the North Pole naturally has no counter or office hours. It is usually the radio operator who doubles as the postmaster and his postal paraphernalia consist of a simple cancellation handstamp, an inking pad and a bottle of ink; all these items can be carried in his pocket.

It would be erroneous to think, however, that the only customers of a North Pole post office are the three or four other members of the expedition. Occasional planes with supplies also bring in letters from all over the world in which philatelists ask for a cancellation by favour because they want to have a letter handled by a North Pole office. Such mail, in fact, comes very often to all post offices operating in high northern or southern latitudes or on board Soviet and U.S. nuclear ice-breakers. Although many such letters have already found their way into philatelic collections, the demand remains permanently high. A true philatelist, however, cannot be very satisfied with a letter bearing a North Pole cancellation because he surely must known that the letter was simply carried by air to a regular mainland head office.

More interesting are genuine letters from remote island and mainland village offices. Their envelopes may bear only ordinary calendar cancellations, or possibly also a few transit postmarks on the back, but a thorough study of literature and other sources will often allow the owner to trace a complicated and unusual delivery or carrier. In the space allotted in this book it is impossible to list all the carriers used by various authorities to deliver ordinary mail back to civilization. It is up to the philatelist to play detective and trace the exciting journey of his letter. Only then will he realize that what he has in his collection is in fact a message passed on like a baton in a relay race by a number of people under most unusual conditions and circumstances.

Our excursion into the world of polar postal services would be incomplete without a brief glance at the opposite side of the globe. Whereas there are many settlements and even cities beyond the Arctic Circle and the exploration and extraction of the vast natural resources of the far north have had a long tradition, Antarctica still remains largely unmapped. Scientists agree that Antarctica is a continent and that there are rich deposits of valuable raw materials under a thick pall of ice and snow. They even managed to map the outline of the continent, but then the politicians and diplomats took over and divided this no-man's land into sectors, declared them their countries' spheres of interest and started to guard the white wastes with great jealousy. The reason is perhaps the region's enormous natural riches but they lie under an armour of ice so thick that even modern sophisticated technology cannot extract them economically. Even to guard one's sector is quite difficult if not impossible. To keep a permanent naval force in the area is uneconomic and land bases would not be able to police much of the territory.

However, the countries involved have found a deft solution: they have established post offices in their territory as a symbol of their sovereignty. After all, the post is a peaceful organization that nobody can have any objection to, and the funds necessary for the support of a single postmaster with a cancellation stamp are negligible. And thus post offices of home countries lying thousands of miles away have been established on various islands off the ice-bound continent as well as on the coast. At first glance these post offices may seem superfluous and their postmaster in danger of being bored to death because the few scientific bases with their mail can hardly keep the Antarctic posts busy. And this is where philatelists come in. Letters from collectors from various countries arrive at these post offices requesting the postmaster to postmark the inserted letters or postcards and send them to the addresses provided. And even though some of these offices are visited by a ship only once or twice a year, philatelists are willing to wait in order to have their wish fulfilled.

Today, however, cancelled letters will wait for a long time only in the smallest and most remote stations and the ship that comes to pick up the mail usually takes away the postmaster who is replaced by somebody else, while by contrast the large bases enjoy more or less regular air connections with home. And as the bases become more and more accessible, philatelists have a unique chance to document postally the advance of civilization into the heartland of the still mysterious continent.

Early Airmail Letters

In 1909 the French aviator Louis Blériot became the first man to fly a plane across the English Channel. His feat was widely acclaimed throughout the world. Naturally, the French were most enthusiastic about the possibilities that Blériot's success seemed to have opened up. They organized the Great Champagne Aviation Week and issued a special airmail promotion label to be affixed on letters that the pilots were to carry in their planes that still flew only short distances. The label bore a picture of a biplane soaring above the Rhine and the post issued a hexagonal cancellation with the date August 29, 1909, and the text *Bethény-Aviation-Marne*. Today, letters with this cancellation and label are considered priceless cornerstones of any airmail collection.

Cancellations of early airmail

Some two years later six and a half thousand letters were flown by the *Allahabad Chamber* biplane from the exhibition grounds in Allahabad, India. The distance that the *Allahabad Chamber* travelled was not too great, either, but the flight represented yet another step forward in the field of mass carriage of mail by air. Other trials soon followed in Great Britain, Italy, South Africa and the U.S.A. In 1917 the Italians opened regular air routes linking Turin with Rome and Naples with Palermo. One year later, the first international route Vienna—Cracow—Lvov—Kiev was opened; philatelic material from these flights ranks among rarities. In 1919 all German

175

post offices started accepting mail for conveyance by air, although this does not mean that air routes connected anything more than a few of the largest cities. The most widely used German route of the time was that from Berlin to Weimar where the Reichstag was in session. A year later the route linking Prague with London via Strasbourg and Paris hopped across half the continent. The planes kept hugging the ground, however, and emergency landings were quite commonplace. Regularity was more of a promotion slogan than a reality.

In 1924 the DERULUFT company, a joint Soviet—German venture, was founded. Its planes flew regularly from Moscow to Königsberg (now Kaliningrad) via Smolensk. Later the route was extended to Berlin. Postage for the flights was paid by the first Soviet official (service) airmail stamp that was nothing but a surcharged old consular issue. The issue is still very popular and much sought on the market.

It was Charles A. Lindbergh with his *Spirit of St. Louis* who made the first solo non-stop transatlantic flight, from New York to Paris in May 1927. This naturally does not mean that most overseas mail was carried by air from that time on. The overwhelming bulk was still carried by ship and pre-war overseas airmail letters constitute valuable additions to any collection.

First Flights

First flights are ventures that take place quite often in various parts of the globe. The name signifies an opening of a new air route, usually an international one, or introduction of a new aicraft on an already existing route. Airlines spend a lot of money to promote the new routes and therefore usually also employ postal cancellations and covers with colourful designs which outline the new route. Since not all international routes are non-stop flights, first flight material may occur in many variants, e.g. letters from the point of departure to various stop-over locations, etc. This means that letters documenting such first flights may bear the stamps and cancellations of different countries. Any philatelist who wants to build a collection documenting the international connections of his national airline, the flights of a specific airline, the density of air routes during a certain period, etc. has a number of alternatives open to him. Although air routes can also be documented on material handled by subsequent regular flights, first flight covers and cancellations prove not only the existence of the route in question but also the date of its opening and are therefore preferred by philatelists.

Helicopter and Rocket Letters

Many airmail letters are decorated with postmarks or labels depicting a helicoper. Conveyance of mail by helicopter is often one of the chief attractions at major festivals, exhibitions, trade fairs, etc.; and since helicopter mail is not so commonplace, philatelists are greatly interested in letters marked as helicopter mail. The first regular international helicopter mail route was opened between The Hague, Holland, and Brussels, Belgium, in 1949.

Any collector who studies philatelic literature and sources will soon find that many postal authorities use helicopters quite routinely, without leaving any postmark or cachet on the envelope. Helicopters are used either on short runs, e.g. linking a G.P.O. with the airport, or to carry mail and supplies to places that are difficult to reach by other means. For instance, since 1972 mail to a high-altitude research station in the Pamirs, Central Asia, has been delivered by helicopter. Formerly, all cargo and mail had to be carried on horseback and each trip took several days. Helicopters are also used to deliver mail in the Arctic, especially to scientific expeditions and prospecting parties working in the field, or in high mountains, deep jungles and other remote places. A collector who notices only the explicit data on an envelope will often fail to recognize a truly unique postal document. If the address sounds the least bit promising or interesting, it may well pay to investigate how the letter actually reached its destination.

Somewhat different are rocket letters. Stamp agencies and shops in many countries have them for sale in large numbers but such letters are primarily designed for profit because rockets have no practical use in postal traffic and it will probably still take some time before missiles can be used economically for the conveyance of mail. Rocket letters sold over the counter and often cluttering up good collections are in most cases mere commercial merchandise produced by extravagantly promoted flights of no practical use, rather than documents from bona fide experiments. Letters from such commercial flights are more often than not decorated with all kinds of colourful labels, handstamps and signatures, but in fact the cartridge containing the mail in most cases flew only a few hundred yards or a few miles at best. Once the cartridge lands, the letters are sold or prepaid with postage and handled normally like any other mail.

The first experiments with bulk transportation of mail by rockets took place in the early 1930s in Austria. The Austrian post launched 24 rockets carrying the total of 6000 letters. In 1939 Cuba launched postal rockets and issued rocket mail stamps but the entire venture never amounted to more than an experiment.

Wreck Letters

First a clarification of the term is perhaps called for since some philatelists wrongly use it to denote mail that must be delivered to areas struck by natural disasters like heavy rains, floods, snow storms, earthquakes, etc. The means of conveyance are often very unusual or unorthodox. In the past, mail and relief food or medicine used to be dropped by parachutes but today's helicopters can either land in the area or hover in the air and lower the cargo by winch. Generally speaking, during emergencies of this kind postal authorities usually have no time to mark mail with the unorthodox manner of delivery and, besides, such mail is better termed as disaster mail.

Most collectors use the term wreck letter for mail that bears a visible proof of having been salvaged from a wreck, e.g. fished from the sea, salvaged from a sunken ship, etc. Such letters often reveal blurred or almost illegible addresses and postal detectives spend a lot of time and effort in order to identify the addressee or at least the sender and sometimes even have to resort to opening the letter in search of a clue.

Another arch enemy of mail is fire. A fire in a post office building, a mail packet or a mail train will result in a pile of burnt letters. Since aircraft have become regular postal carriers, philatelic collections have been enriched by letters termed sometimes separately as Air Accident Covers that bear traces of aircraft wrecks. At best the letters may be merely wrinkled or soiled if the salvaging teams collected them in the fields, forests and even fished them from the lakes near the site of the accident. In more severe cases the letters may be partially incinerated. According to international custom, the salvaging administration places identified mail in transparent envelopes with a brief note attached that gives the place and time of the wreck, and frequently also an apology for delayed delivery and damage, and forwards them to identified delivery addresses.

Wreck letters are very popular among collectors who build entire specialized collections. Letters salvaged from certain much publicized wrecks are more valued than mail from local accidents, regardless of the extent of damage. For example, greatly valued among philatelists are letters salvaged from the wreck of the *Hindenburg* (LZ 129) at Lakehurst, New Jersey, or from the fire of a Transcanadian Express train.

Dog Team Letters

Dog teams used to be employed for mail delivery in the North, i.e. Canada, Alaska and Siberia. Modern transportation means have superseded dog teams so that dog team letters are quite rare nowadays. If used at all, dog teams represent a temporary makeshift solution that is sooner or later replaced by airscrew-driven sledges, helicopters, snowcats (ratracks) or snowmobiles. Unfortunately for philatelists, those few dog team routes that still remain in operation do not mark specially the mail carried and philatelists who are interested in such mail are best advised to study professional newsletters, information bulletins and official gazettes for information concerning mail carriers used in the Arctic regions.

In 1908 there existed a regular privately operated Canadian dog team route nicknamed the MacGreel Express. The post used its own cancellations and postage stamps. Another popular route, called the Dog Team Post, operated in Alaska. The route had relay stations where mail was accepted for handling. The stations were about 75 km apart, a distance which equalled a day trip of a dog team.

At the end of the 19th century, dog team posts operated also in Russia, especially around Lake Baikal and on the Kamchatka. Usually three sledges travelled together, each pulled by 8—10 pack dogs and a leader dog. Apart from the mail, a dog driver and a postal clerk, dog teams sometimes also carried a single passenger. Collecting dog team letters is very popular especially among American philatelists.

Pony Express

Prior to the opening of the Panama Canal, ships could reach San Francisco from New York only by way of Cape Horn and the voyage was rough and took several months. While the states of the Atlantic seaboard and the Midwest as well as California saw a rapid development of industry and growth of population, the Great Plains still remained only sparsely populated by Indian tribes and roamed by huge herds of buffalo. Overland communications by means of a prairie schooner drawn by a team of horses or oxen were extremely slow and dangerous because of Indians and white outlaws alike. The situation could be improved only by a railway but the construction of a transcontinental link was a lengthy project. Yet a solution had to be found immediately because the discovery of gold in California in the 1840s made more and more people leave the populous eastern states and go west.

All these people wanted to communicate with teir families, friends and companies back east, required many things ranging from nails to guns and wanted all of them quickly. This need provided an impulse for the establishment of several express mail and freight companies whose wagons carried gold on their way back. Mail was prepaid by regular U.S. postage and an extra fee was levied by the companies that carried the letters over hundreds of miles of wilderness. The best-known of these firms was Wells, Fargo and Co. Its heavy wagons rolled along only very slowly and deliveries took up to three months. Therefore in 1860 the stagecoach and freighting firm of Russell, Majors and Waddell established a special fast mail route operated by experienced express riders. The route linked St. Joseph, Missouri, whrere the railway ended, with Sacramento, California. Pony Express riders covered the distance of 2000 miles (3200 km) in nine days and a letter posted in New York could reach San Francisco in 12 or 13 days in this way.

The Pony Express has entered the annals of postal history as one of the most dangerous routes of all times. For a weekly pay of U.S. $ 25 the firm offered employment to young men seeking adventure. Their job was to carry four saddle bags with 10—15 kg of mail and to ride as fast as possible to the next relay station. The stations were spaced some 10—15 miles apart and provided the riders with fresh horses. The rider had only to resaddle and hurry on; company rules stipulated that changing a saddle should not take more than two minutes.

One of the most famous riders of the Pony Express service was William Cody who had started his colourful career as a horseman at the tender age of fifteen. During the Civil War he served as a scout for the Union troops, then he was hired by the railroad company as a buffalo hunter to supply fresh meat to construction workers laying the transcontinental railway and that is where he won his famous nickname, Buffalo Bill. The Pony Express service remained in business for about 18 months and carried some 35,000 articles during that period. The postage was quite high: the basic fee for a half-ounce (i.e. 14.17 g) letter was 5 dollars, with a dollar extra for each additional half-ounce.

The Pony Express ultimately become such a legend that in 1940 the U.S. Mails honoured it with a commemorative issue depicting a Pony Express rider. Besides the Pony Express there were also other services of this kind like the Mustang Express, Hanford's Pony Express, etc. Between them, these services delivered hundreds of thousands of letters. Although most have not survived, collectors even today may come across specimens that travelled the hard and dangerous overland journey in the box of a slow-moving stagecoach or in a saddlebag of a galloping Pony Express.

Mailcoach Letters

Prior to the invention of the railway, the main means of postal transportation was a heavy mailcoach drawn by a team of four. The difficult-to-manoeuvre mailcoaches criss-crossed Europe, negotiated the American Great Plains, provided postal service for remote Siberian settlements and travelled across the Australian deserts.

Even today letters can be carried by mailcoach; in fact collectors are willing to pay extra sums to be able to send their letters by this slow and ancient means of transportation. Modern mailcoaches naturally leave an imprint on letters in the form of special and commemorative postmarks and labels. Special mailcoach services are operated to commemorate the anniversaries of cities, various events and to promote trade fairs, large agricultural exhibitions and folk festivals. Children's villages in Austria and West Germany have capitalized on the popularity of the ancient stagecoach among philatelists and the charity that runs these villages has made an agreement with the local authority which permits it to have a certain number of letters carried by these historical vehicles. Perhaps the longest modern mailcoach service was operated in Poland on the occasion of the 500th anniversary of the birth of the great astronomer Nicholas Copernicus. The mailcoach travelled through a large part of the country, visiting cities that had played an important role in Copernicus' life and career. All municipal postal offices en route accepted mail for handling using commemorative cancellations, so that a diligent collector could gather some twenty different postal documents from this single route alone.

Despite all the promotion given in philatelic magazines and by philatelic businesses to these souvenirs, and regardless of the fact that this type of merchandise is legitimized by postal authorities that imprint it with regular posting or arrival cancellations, letters of this kind represent nothing but philatelic gimmicks with practically no collector's value, although the selling price may be quite high. Actually the post does not need such commemorative events to remain in business; in fact the reverse is true because these ventures only slow the postal operations down.

Although in some countries horse teams with wagons still provide certain auxiliary services, unfortunately for collectors, such carriers are not marked on the covers in any way.

Wandering Letters

As the bulk of mail handled continually grows, as more and more people need to keep in contact with friends and associates abroad, as travel becomes progressively easier, the volume of wandering letters grows, too. This type of letter is not difficult to recognize because it invariably has a lot of postmarks, notes and penmarks that often fill not only the face side but in fact all free space on the envelope. The existence of wandering letters is caused, for instance, by an incorrectly written address or because the addressee has moved without leaving a forwarding address or by an error on the part of the sender. Such letters wander from city to city, and sometimes from country to country and even from continent to continent, depending on the geographical knowledge of the clerk handling such a letter with an incomplete or unclear address. The situation is sometimes aggravated by the fact that many places have the same name at home or even abroad (for example, there are three Newports in the U.K. and two in the U.S.A.). More prosaically there may be several streets with the same name in a city so that if the sender forgets to write the district or writes it incorrectly the letter may travel for weeks or even months.

Every post office that finds itself with such an undeliverable letter will make an investigation in its postal delivery district, mark the result on the envelope, stamp it and submit the letter to its head office. The number of undeliverables due to incorrect or incomplete addresses can be perhaps somewhat decreased when postal delivery codes (ZIP codes) are used universally, especially for international mail. Very difficult to deliver are also letters addressed to people who permanently change their residence, e.g. for business reasons, and even move from country to country as their job requires. Such letters end up so covered with various postmarks, handstamps and penmarks that the original mailing address is hardly legible anymore.

A somewhat different case is presented by letters that the sender himself — usually a collector — dispatches with several forwarding addresses because he wants the letter to travel to various parts of the world before having it returned. Such circulation letters were quite common at the end of the last century. Then there are letters mailed by the sender first to the North and then to the South Pole because the collector wants to have two cancellations from the opposite ends of the world impressed side by side on a single cover. Such letters often return only after several years. Philatelists can sometimes see these 'documents' at stamp exhibitions but one should remember that such artificialities have no place in a serious collection. On the other hand, an unintentionally wandering letter will always be an interesting proof of the diligent and painstaking work of the post.

Hotel Posts

The first private posts of alpine hotels and chalets in Austria and Switzerland originated at the end of the 19th century. Hotel posts were also later established in other countries with a large tourist trade. In contrast to private urban posts that sprang up approximately at the same time in many European cities, state postal authorities recognized hotel posts as their partners and helpers rather than competitors. The problem was that state posts often could not guarantee delivery to every remote hotel or chalet high in the mountains and therefore considered its duty fulfilled if the mail was dropped in the hotel box at the local office. When somebody from the hotel came down into town he picked up the mail and took it back. Large hotels in mountain resorts therefore established private hotel posts with messengers who walked during summer and used skis in the winter. The messengers took care of the communications between the individual hotels in the area and also provided the link with the state post. Hotel posts levied small fees for their services and the payment was certified by private labels.

Since hotel posts provided contacts with the state-run post, there are letters bearing hotel stamps as well as state issues. The construction of alpine roads, cableways and utilization of modern means of transportation by postal services gradually rendered hotel posts superfluous.

Postal Wars

The Convention of the Universal Postal Union declares that no stamp or other postal issue must display a text or a design that could be offensive to public morals or the national sentiment, political creed or system of any UPU member state. However, there have been violations of the rule that resulted in a protest by the offended country and even in a ban on mail bearing the offensive issue. In such cases sorting offices are ordered to mark the offensive article with a handstamp stating that the used issue is not permitted in the destination country or with a stamp referring to the relevant article of the Convention. The letter is then returned to the posting country. Other authorities simply defend their country's honour by blackening the undesirable stamp and levying fines by means of a postage due stamp. In some cases rubber stamps are replaced by labels explaining why the letter cannot be accepted for handling.

There have also been cases when the answer came not from the post but from the country's generals who started rattling their hardware. In 1900 the Dominican Republic, a country occupying a portion of the Caribbean island of Hispaniola, issued a stamp featuring a map of the island. Whether by intent or through shoddy work on the part of the designer is not known but the fact remains that the miniature map showed a part of the neighbouring Republic of Haiti incorporated in the Dominican Republic. The Haitians naturally considered the stamp an outrage and many hotheads called for revenge. The other party did not want to be caught unprepared and also started sabre-rattling. Luckily enough a few sensible politicians opened negotiations and the incident was settled without a single shot being fired; the offensive issue was officially incinerated.

Between the world wars, the postal authorities of Poland and the Free City of Danzig used their stamps to exchange their views on history which were very contradictory.

Another case of a postal war concerned the interests of Great Britain and Chile which clashed in Antarctica. As we have said before, scientists believe there to be enormous deposits of strategic raw materials under the armour of ice covering the sixth continent. Although economically and technologically unable to extract these riches, several countries rushed to establish their sectors in Antarctica. And thus in 1940 the Chilean President signed a decree that proclaimed a part of Antarctica to be Chilean territory. Five years later a Chilean scientific expedition was much surprised to find a British expedition operating in Chilean Antarctic Teritory. Chile thought this an insult to Chilean sovereignty and decided in 1947 to remind the world of its rights by issuing postage stamps with a design to that effect. Great Britain understood the Chilean intent only too well but was not ready to yield to unilateral claims and did not withdraw its expedition from the disputed territory. As a counter measure, Britain issued its own stamps that showed the Falkland Islands and the same Antarctic Territory as British possessions. The outraged Chilean Government sent an official note of protest to London and at the same time dispatched a small naval force to patrol the Antarctic coast. However, the upkeep of troops in Antarctica was too expensive and after aimlessly patrolling the deserted coast the Chilean Navy sailed home and the international conflict petered out without having been resolved. Needless to say, neither side withdrew the stamps.

Somewhat worse was the outcome of a stamp war between two Central American republics, Nicaragua and Honduras.

In 1937 Nicaragua issued an airmail stamp showing Nicaraguan territory to be so large that neighbouring Honduras took it as an act of aggression without a formal declaration of war. Luckily, its armed forces did not retaliate immediately. The Honduran government first asked Nicaragua to apologize and take the offensive issue out of circulation. Nicaragua refused, the situation became critical and both countries dispatched troops to the common border. While mobilization was going on, the two countries opened negotiations which ultimately resolved nothing but at least it was arguments that were exchanged rather than fire. As time went by, the troops at the border remained on alert but tempers began to subside. In the end Honduras decided to boycott the issue and banned letters bearing the offending stamp from its territory. Nicaragua never invalidated the stamps but since most of its airmail went to Honduras, Nicaraguans started to boycott the stamp as well because it was of no use to them. The stamp soon ceased to be sold, the cause of the conflict was forgotten and the troops were withdrawn. The financial costs of the postal war have never been calculated.

By far the worst situation arose from a similar conflict between Paraguay and its neighbour Bolivia. In 1932 Paraguay issued a stamp of its territory which showed the Gran Chaco as incorporated in Paraguay. Gran Chaco was a part of Bolivia and that country dispatched an official protest. However, Paraguay replied rather arrogantly and Bolivia mobilized its troops. Paraguay followed suit and the conflict over a postage stamp grew into a real war, with soldiers killed on both sides who had perhaps never even seen the stamp that caused their deaths. The short but bloody war was lost by Bolivia, which had to cede the Chaco to Paraguay.

Stamps may cause ill feelings between countries that normally enjoy good diplomatic relations or are even allies. For example, Italy after the Second World War issued stamps that promoted the tour of the Italian president in Latin America, only to destroy the entire issue because a few minor but incorrect details caused ill will on the part of the countries involved. There have also been some more recent Western European issues that caused considerable ill feelings in Eastern Europe. As a rule, mail with these stamps was returned with a note quoting the UPU regulations.

Czechoslovakia issued a stamp with an engraving of Picasso's famous *Guernica*. General Franco was still alive then and, although Picasso himself hailed the engraving as an outstanding artistic achievement, letters from Czechoslovakia bearing the stamp offensive to the Franco regime were banned from Spain; the ban was lifted only after General Franco's death.

As we have seen, stamps have been the cause of many postal conflicts and even wars and it is only natural that such issues will always be in the foreground of collectors' interest.

Inflation Letters

Every period of hyper-inflation (when prices rise by a minimum of 50 % a month) is philatelically very interesting although not only for the exorbitant sums that have to be paid for ordinary postage. Letters bearing stamps with face values in the order of hundreds, thousands, millions and even billions naturally appear very attractive and if the printing houses managed to issue them in time to cover the prescribed postage, letters bearing such stamps were handled quite normally. This is an early stage in the economic whirlwind when the post, the stamp printing bureaux and the customers can all still act in accordance with the existing regulations. Then follows a much more complicated stage when prices rise at such an astronomical rate that the post cannot keep up because it has no time to prepare stamps of the required face value. Improvisation becomes the order of the day and the post is forced to resort to various emergency measures and produce 'provisionals' (i.e. stamps that are not authorized by postal regulations). Later collectors can document the character of the times on the basis of a host of unusual inflationary issues.

To document the rising mail rates is quite easy; in fact relevant data for all inflationary periods can be found in stamp catalogues. Collectors can look up the rates for various mail classes applicable for each stage of the inflation and gather material to document the inflation spiral. However, sooner or later they will come across material of a more unusual character, e.g. stamps manufactured in the period when postages lagged behind the inflation rate and extra sheets of paper had to be attached to letters to provide enough space for all the stamps required.

As was said before, the advanced stages of inflation necessarily called for improvisations and local measures and this is precisely where a philatelist becomes a detective who traces and documents in his collection phenomena that are not always recorded in catalogues: various kinds of provisional labels with hand-written sums that had to be paid in cash at the counter; crude makeshift receipts for astronomical sums; proofs that a stamp was given a face value exceeding the original denomination by several orders of decimal. Hyper-inflation was usually marked by general chaos and confusion and even postal clerks themselves could not be sure what rates were applicable at any given moment. To attempt to document all these things on different mail issued by different posts is an exciting challenge for any collector. Actually, the number of possible varieties of even a single issue can be staggering as we have seen in the example of the inflationary issue of Azerbaijan discussed earlier in this book.

A lot pf philatelically fascinating material can be found also among postal documents of European countries boasting of a long postal and printing tradition. German inflation letters affixed with entire sections of stamp printing sheets worth a billion marks are quite commonplace in collections. Incidentally, the highest denomination German issue is a 1923 stamp showing the figure of 59 billion marks. Less then thirty years later inflation in Hungary was responsible for an issue with the face value of 500,000,000,000,000,000 pengö. These and similar figures are completely staggering and it is not surprising that such historic inflationary issues have remained a popular collection theme.

During inflation, rotary printing presses running 24 hours a day printed stamps of huge denominations. And yet as the stamps were leaving the printing plant the post could

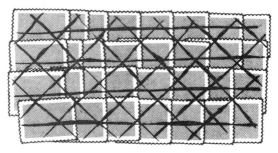

So-called roof postage from the period inflation in Germany

not be sure that the sum would be high enough to cover the postage. It was a common experience that the authorities hat to withdraw freshly printed stamps to have them immediately surcharged with a still higher figure. Surcharges of this type are a characteristic feature of all inflationary issues and philatelists should be aware that unused inflationary stamps are mere minimum-value prints and that only their actual use on a letter, i.e. a proof that they were accepted by the post, gives them a real value. Used inflationary stamps are therefore philatelically more valuable than unused ones.

One should beware of subsequent fake cancellations featuring forged or altered dates. Any collector who intends to devote his collection to an inflationary period of a particular country should first study the catalogues and relevant literature or consult an expert. There are experts specializing in European inflationary stamps (those of Germany, Austria, Hungary, Romania, Free City of Danzig, etc.) whose certificate of genuineness on the stamp will enable a collector to include the stamp in his collection without any reservation. However, the most interesting documents from the uneasy inflationary periods are entires showing some irregularity. The greater the latter, the better the philatelic value and therefore also the price, but also the greater the danger of the entire being a forgery. Consulting an expert, especially in the case of higher-priced entires, is always advisable.

Letters from Concentration Camps

After the Second World War many philatelic exhibitions displayed entire collections of letters, postcards and lettercards, mostly written in heavy script and primitive German on pre-printed forms. The world philatelic press soon opened discussions about the formal aspects of such mail and various official preprinted correspondence forms. During the war several hundred concentration camps existed in Nazi-held territories but the regulations concerning the inmates' mail were not uniform and changed often even in a single camp, so that there could be several forms used in the same camp over the years. Correspondence from police jails was usually written on ordinary postcards. Such mail naturally bears also the ubiquitous censorship rubber stamps or penmarks. The location can be established either from the sender's address or from the contents of the message.

Rules regulating the incoming correspondence for inmates in Nazi penitentiaries and concentration camps were quite different. The censor was usually obliged to make sure that the paper under the stamp did not bear a coded message and stamps were therefore roughly torn off and often damaged in the process, leaving only remnants pasted to the envelope. In spite of the damage philatelists regard such mail as full-value material documenting the period character. On the other hand, letters addressed to concentration camps that have their stamps intact should be regarded with caution. In some cases the incoming mail had to be addressed to the Jewish Elders, a body residing outside the camp proper and established to make the camps look like self-governing institutions. There the incoming mail was collected, delivered in the camp, censored by the authorities and distributed.

The concentration camp in Terezín (Ger. Theresienstadt), where entire families including children were imprisoned before selection and transportation to extermination camps such as Auschwitz, was first so flooded with incoming parcels that the German authorities had to impose certain restrictions on the mail privileges of the inmates. An order for an issue of admission stamps was placed with Prague's State Printing Bureau and the Elders were given a limited number of the stamps to send to addresses provided by the inmates. Further parcels were accepted for handling only if they bore these special admission stamps. They were obliterated postally by ordinary cancellations. Naturally, entire package wrappers including the stamps or at least wrapper cut-squares are philatelic rarities today and fetch much higher prices on the market than unused admission stamps. However, since many stamps with fake cancellations cropped up after the war, collectors are best advised to consult an expert.

Since the Theresienstadt camp was visited several times by a delegation of the International Red Cross, the authorities, who wanted to impress the representatives favourably, had souvenir sheets of the admission stamps printed from the original plate. The issue was quite limited in number and many forgeries including some very crude ones appeared on the market after the war. Just before the war ended the printing plate was taken away from the Bureau by a high-ranking SS officer who disappeared with it and the plates were never found again. At the last minute, however, the engraver was able to make a small but visible mark on the plate so that any speculative reprints should they ever appear, could be told apart from the original issue. Again, collectors are advised to consult specialized literature.

The Jewish Elders of the concentration camp in Litzmanstadt even printed a camp post issue with the approval of the camp command. However, permission was then withdrawn and the entire issue was confiscated, although how many stamps reached the market after the war is now impossible to tell. The stamps are listed in some specialized catalogues and there are dealers who occasionally advertise specimens for high prices. The only thing that an expert can do in this case is to compare the individual specimens and see which printing is better or more precise although no one will be probably able to tell which print, if any, dates from the time of the stamp's origin.

The volume of philatelic material from the period is quite considerable and a diligent collector would be able to build an interesting collection from concentration camp letters and stamps. It should be borne in mind, however, that this type of mail is becoming more and more scarce and that almost all specimens from families' correspondence have already found their way into philatelic collections.

Electronic Letters

Today, TV frequencies are used to transmit letters from place to place via communication satellites. In the receiving station the 'letter' is automatically transcribed onto paper, placed in an envelope and delivered by traditional methods to the addressee. Such letters cover the major part of their journey in a matter of seconds and if the rest of the journey is swift enough, the letter can reach its destination on the same day it is dispatched, which is indeed a fantastic pace because even airmail takes several days to deliver.

Another sophisticated electronic means of communication of various written or printed matter including blueprints is facsimile transmission using telephone or telex carriers. The advantage is that the communication does not have to go through a post office but can be directly transmitted via an exchange to a receiver hooked up to a private subscriber line.

Of course, this type of service is rather expensive for private subscribers but large firms use facsimile equipment routinely. Postally handled electronic letters have still not found their way in philatelic collections but any future exhibition may reflect the sophisticated level of modern postal services.

Space Letters

Space post has been a reality for a number of years, and the philatelic public all over the world has been able to see exhibits of mail delivered to and from space as well as equipment used in temporary post offices aboard spacecraft. The Space Museum in Star City near Moscow displays the first mail delivered from orbit; there are not only official communications but also private correspondence and even newspapers. Both Soviet cosmonauts and American astronauts leaving for missions in space are authorized by their postal administrations to act as postal agents and supplied with the necessary paraphernalia such as cancellation stamps, labels, etc. The U.S. Mails has even had a special leather bag made for this purpose which has already travelled several times in space.

Although mail has been delivered to and from spacecraft, special space post stamps have not been issued yet and philatelists will probably have to wait before space correspondence is included in ordinary collections. Nevertheless, letters that have allegedly been in space and are even stamped to that effect are sold from time to time at much publicized auctions for great sums of money. The matter has been widely discussed by the philatelic press and it seems that an enterprising European dealer specializing in airmail letters managed to pull off a fantastic business coup. He made a surreptitious deal with a U.S. astronaut who agreed to take along about one hundred unofficial letters on his next space mission, naturally for a large fee. The letters obviously could not be addressed to anybody in space; in fact the dealer needed them back to be able to capitalize on them. When the spacecraft reached the farthest point from Earth, the astronaut stamped the letters with a special cancellation he had been provided with and countersigned it. Before landing he hid the letters among his personal effects. A scandal broke out and NASA fired the astronaut. Perhaps his fee covered even such eventuality. The letters change hands from time to time but their buyers can be hardly called philatelists because such letters have nothing in common with postal services or true philately.

A PERFECT STAMP

Obviously, a stamp with its cancellation must be genuine to start with to be worthy of a collection. But even two identical, genuine stamps may have different philatelic values and therefore also prices. The differences are based on philatelic qualities but what actually are the requirements that a stamp must meet to deserve a permanent place in a collection?

First of all, it must not be damaged. By damage we mean not only a large cut in the design but even a minutely split edge, a small tear discernible only if the stamp is closely inspected, or a single missing perforation tooth torn off by careless separation from the sheet. Missing corner perforation teeth often result in rounded corners.

All this does not imply, however, that a stamp that is in a less than one hundred per cent condition must be immediately rejected or scrapped. Especially if it is a rarity, one need not be so strict, although whenever a chance arises to obtain a better specimen the defective stamp should be replaced. Obviously, imperfect specimens have a lower selling and exchange value.

Neither should the stamp be holed in any way unless the perforation was required by the issuing authority or wholesale buyer as a proof of cancellation or prevention against unauthorized use. In the past, many collectors rejected perfins, which are produced by various business firms or official agencies to prevent the use of company postage for private correspondence. The opposite seems to be true today as regards perfins and entire collections composed solely of perfins are now being built up and collectors try to trace all companies that have used perfin stamps; in fact some perfins have greatly gained in popularity. For example, recently there has been a great demand on the market for German stamps bearing POL perfins and denoting stamps that used to be the property of police.

Stamps can have defects that are difficult to recognize at first glance. Damage can be caused by inexpert or hasty removal from the cover which results in tearing off a part of the back of the stamp. Stamps with this type of defect are known as 'thinned' and will remain undetected unless viewed against light; thinner spots will appear lighter on inspection. Briefly, the stamp paper should be perfect not only on the face but also on the back.

However, many readers will know that the most expensive stamp in the world, the famous 1856 British Guiana, is itself defective. Every philatelist knows that the stamp was originally rectangular and yet the only surviving specimen is an octagon because somebody cut its four corners off. The answer is really very simple: its defects are beside the point because there is only one specimen left in the whole world and its uniqueness makes it priceless.

Stamps are sometimes treated by stamp doctors who can repair them so skilfully that a thin spot is very difficult to find, or attach a missing perforation tooth or retouch a surface scratch. The services of these experts are very expensive and cosmetic touches like this are better left to especially valuable or rare stamps. Besides, regardless of the treatment, a doctored stamp can never be a one hundred per cent specimen. Although the treatment may considerably improve the appearance so that the stamp can be included in a collection, the fact that it has been doctored must not be concealed and prospective buyers are fully within their right to ask for a price discount. Any expert asked to certify the stamp must state in his certificate that it has been reconditioned.

However, the situation with classic imperforate issues is much more complicated. The margins may sometimes differ in width, or the stamp may even have a cut in the design. The wider the margin on all sides, the higher the value of the stamp. If a rare classic is partially damaged by a cut that even a stamp

Reconditioning of thinned stamps with paper mass

clinic cannot fix, it would be a pity not to include the stamp in a collection although it can never be passed as perfect.

But even if the paper of a stamp is in good condition, perforated stamps may be improperly centred. The design may be shifted so that the print is closer to one side than to the other. The defect of these *off centres* is caused by an imperfect positioning of the stamp sheet in the perforating machine, or by an inaccurate adjustment of the latter. A one hundred per cent specimen must be aligned dead centre.

Another factor that will lower the value of an otherwise perfect stamp is the cancellation. As a rule, no stamp with a blurred, smudged or greasy-like cancellation should be included in a good collection. Yet even if the cancellation is applied neatly and covers only a minor part of the stamp the collector may still not be too happy about it. A perfect stamp should bear a cancellation that is legible, unless it is a mute one. Cancellations forming a mere arc in a stamp corner should be judged as suspicious, especially in those cases when a used specimen has a higher value than an unused one. Such cancellations may be faked and, even if the specimen in question was cancelled later by a genuine cancellation, it still remains a fake. Classic cancellations forming two concentric circles should have a legible centre showing the number of the post office that cancelled the stamp. Many philatelists use these cancellations to document entire old postal networks and long-distance routes. A perfect cancellation on a perfect stamp should look as if neatly drawn. Anybody who has ever seen exhibits in the honour class of a major exhibition will agree that owners of these collections must have spent a lot of time and often money before they came across perfect specimens for their collection, although their issues are frequently more than a century old.

While discussing stamp qualities we should not forget the attributes of other collection material, namely postcards. The rules concerning stamp cancellations apply also to those found on postcards. Apart from that, it should be borne in mind that postal stationery can crumple, crease, soil or lose corners easily and that damaged specimens always lower the aesthetic value of any collection.

Remember that carelessly or hastily opened envelopes will tear along the edge. If a torn edge cannot be corrected by a slight trim, it is better to fix it with a transparent adhesive tape. Some collectors wrongly think that it is only the address side that matter on covers and therefore often cut the back off. Such envelopes cease to be worthy of their name and remain mere cut-squares on which it is impossible to ascertain whether they also carried arrival cancellations, transit postmarks, pen-marks made by censors or delivery postmen, or any other facts about their handling. A cut-square usually has a lower collector value than an entire. However, if an envelope has no other valuable feature than a mere commemorative or special cancellation then it is better to reduce it to a cut-square. The space in the album normally required to hold an entire can be better used for mounting two or three such cut-squares. This lends the collection a more compact character. These and other aspects will be discussed in the chapter on the arrangement of a collection.

FORGERIES: A GREAT HEADACHE

Unfortunately, there are many philatelic forgeries in circulation. Primarily, they are made to defraud collectors of classics although they need not always be forgeries of highly priced stamps, because a skilful forger can often make a nice profit even on lower-priced stamps, especially if they are not too difficult to counterfeit. Sometimes it is enough to alter the colour slightly or simply to make a photograph of a genuine specimen to produce an autotype and to print easily any number of copies that will fetch a tidy sum on the market. To make fake cancellations or to remove them chemically or to apply gum on the back of a stamp is even easier. Of course, total forgeries of old stamps are much more difficult to make but expert forgers can cope even with such technically sophisticated jobs.

As we have said before, there are many forged stamps in circulation that look so perfect that even an experienced collector is sometimes ready to swear that they are genuine. Forgeries can be basically of two types: postal forgeries (Fr. *faux pour servir*) are made to deceive the post office, i.e. they are used for postage. However, since postal rates are relatively low, it would take a large stock of forged stamps and a long time to make the forgery a profitable venture. Besides, the risk of detection is always quite high. For this reason only a small percentage of all forgeries made are produced to defraud the post.

A much greater profit is to be derived from forgeries aimed at the collector market. Such forgeries are often made in one country and sold in another and even the police are sometimes quite helpless since legislation in many countries does not protect foreign, much less old and invalidated postage issues.

One of the most famous forgery cases of all time took place in France at the beginning of this century. Customs officers in Aix-les-Bains seized a letter addressed to a party living in Italy and containing a number of valuable European classics that were worth a small fortune. The sender of the letter, one Jean de Speratti, insisted that the customs clear the letter, saying that the stamps were not genuine issues but art reproductions. This, incidentally, had been declared on the envelope. But the customs refused to fall for what they considered a cheap trick and went to court. The court summoned experts from among local collectors and their expertise confirmed the customs' original suspicion, i.e. that the confiscated prints were in fact rare stamp issues.

Speratti, who apparently had wanted to avoid paying a high duty, seemed in danger of being found guilty of fraud and sentenced to a heavy fine. And then the defendant shocked the court with his statement that the alleged genuine philatelic rarities were his own work. He even submitted a few originals to the court for comparison and expressed his willingness to demonstrate his skill. Since the confiscated stamps were neither part of a French issue nor valid, Speratti could not even be accused of forgery. There was also no evidence of his ever trying to peddle his work as genuine postage stamps.

Although it may seem far-fetched the fact remains that during the trial the exhibited originals and Speratti's copies were somehow mixed up and even the court experts could not agree which stamps were genuine and which were not. In the end it had to be left to the defendant to decide which was his own work. The public prosecutor refused to give in, the trial dragged on and on and when the defendant was asked why he had taken up such work to start with, Speratti obstinately held that he had done so for study purposes.

Speratti was acquitted and to prove his statement he even wrote a book about his work and announced that he would publish a sampler to go with it. Stamp dealers and owners of classic collections suddenly became afraid because nobody could be sure any more whether the stamps on which they had staked their reputation were genuine. Large philatelic clubs were alerted, meetings of stamp experts were held and as a result the entire stock of Speratti's book was immediately bought up and the promised sampler was never allowed to reach the hands of the public. Speratti actually did not fare too badly, because he was handsomely paid off. Incidentally, he had to promise that he would never again study stamps in such a dangerous manner.

Actually, the Speratti case was not the first one of its kind. Speratti had a predecessor, a Swiss national named Fournier. Fournier differed from all other forgers because he did not intend to spend a lot of time and effort in producing a few forged specimens of rare stamps and to market them illicitly at great risk to himself. He instead decided to help philatelists fill the blank spaces in their albums at reasonable prices. This, however, could be achieved only by large-scale production. Fournier therefore bought a partnership in the Mercier printing company in Geneva and the firm started manufacturing stamp facsimiles. Rare, expensive stamps were printed in whole sheets in staggering numbers. Fournier naturally never made the mistake of trying to pass off his copies as genuine classic rarities. His dealership simply offered collectors a chance to acquire specimens that they lacked in their collections.

In 1910, when Fournier himself could not be sure any more what he had made and marketed, he had a catalogue of his merchandise published. It revealed that the skilful Swiss had marketed copies of more than 1200 rare issues and of 636 surcharges on genuine stamps. However, to put it rather bluntly, what Fournier had done was to flood the world market with forgeries. If at first philatelists had viewed his activities with a benevolent smile, they now began to be frightened by the scope and impact of the whole venture. The original owners of collections padded with Fournier's merchandise who knew where and what they had acquired could die and their heirs would have no idea that they had inherited forgeries that could be passed on undetected. Nobody could be sure if some of the most famous collections were completely genuine. Stamp experts suddenly found themselves in great demand and could not cope with all the extra work. Then during the First World War Fournier died and his heir was only too glad to yield to the wishes of philatelic organizations and sell the inheritance. Facsimiles that the company still had in stock were listed and the Geneva Philatelic Club sent a copy to world-renowned stamp experts and major philatelic organizations. The rest of the stock was then scrapped under official supervision.

Since then the names of Speratti and Fournier have become familiar to every stamp collector. From time to time the two are remembered in the philatelic press and even by large philatelic exhibitions; the Swiss have even turned the Fournier workshop into a museum.

Although the most important aspect of stamp forgery is the technique, which must be as perfect as that employed for the manufacture of the original, another vital factor is the psychological preparation, or brainwashing, of the prospective buyer. This is perhaps best illustrated by another famous forgery case.

Wertheimer-Ghica was an old noble Romanian family. However, Baron Wertheimer-Ghica who lived at the beginning of the century, could boast of nothing but his name because the family wealth had long gone and the baron had to look for some means of support. In the end he hit upon an idea that was as original as it was crooked.

He spent several years in preparation by studying the oldest Romanian, i.e. Moldavian, issues. Although he was poor, his name gained him easy access to various libraries and archives, so that in time he was able to amass a considerable knowledge about the design, manufacture and printing techniques of the oldest Romanian stamps, which are prized by collectors all over the world. He even went so far as to write a couple of short studies on the subject. As a consequence his authority grew in the philatelic world.

Following these first successes he collected his articles in a volume on classic Romanian stamps that won him further acclaim and a firm position as an expert. But the royalties from his writings were not enough to provide a comfortable living for the rest of his life and thus one day Baron Wertheimer-Ghica offered some stamps for sale. Because of his reputation as an expert, the buyers never dreamed that he could sell them worthless forgeries. The deals earned the baron a tidy sum; in fact he could live quite comfortably on the interest alone.

To be sure, Wertheimer-Ghica decided not to wait too long and he left Romania because he correctly presumed that the truth must be revealed sooner or later. And when one of the dealers also wanted to make sure and had the purchased stamps checked by other experts, the baron found himself in trouble. Suddenly more and more buyers were discovering that they had been cheated and Wertheimer-Ghica was soon sought for fraud. However, he was faster than the police and managed to disappear with the money somewhere in Latin America.

At about the same time a young, elegant gentleman accompanied by a secretary checked into a reputable Paris hotel. The olive-skinned faces and hard-to-pronounce names under which the two registered fired the curiosity of the staff. The mysterious guest was difficult to approach since he lived in seclusion in his suite and everybody and everything had to go through his secretary. One day the secretary indiscreetly revealed a piece of information that stunned everybody. The exotic name of the young gentleman was a mere front for His Majesty Maria I, the young sovereign of Se-Dan-Gu, a small kingdom hidden in the remote Himalayan valleys and plateaus near the Chinese border. It seemed that His Majesty was travelling incognito to be in a better position to see life in Europe, should his real identity be revealed, he would have to depart immediately.

Needless to say, the management and the staff of the hotel were delighted to have such a distinguished exotic monarch among their guests and the suite of the elegant, ever-smiling foreigner became the centre of the staff's attention. Then one day the chambermaids spotted an envelope with an exotic-looking stamp lying in the waste-paper basket. Used envelopes in waste-paper baskets are nothing out of the ordinary in a big hotel but this one was rather special since it had passed through the hands of a sovereign of a remote Himalayan kingdom!

And thus the envelope, which was soon followed by others, ended up in the hands of stamp dealers. A few well-placed hints here and there made the exotic stamps a very sought-after commodity among speculators. The hotel lobby was suddenly full of people looking for ways to penetrate the mysterious suite.

In the end the suave secretary agreed to see a few of the most importunate entrepreneurs. Smiles and expensive gifts were exchanged for vague promises. Finally the dealers were rewarded for having been so patient and generous: His Majesty graciously consented to have some of his country's stamps sold. The secretary divided the lot among the most generous dealers. All in all, the deal was worth almost a million francs. All transactions were kept secret in order to protect the king's incognito and to exclude competition.

Nobody will ever know who first decided to take a good look at the map to try and locate the mysterious kingdom but the fact remains that one day too many people were interested in the far, exotic land nobody knew anything about. The kingdom was not to be found and neither was the king. His Majesty and his secretary checked out in such haste that they even forgot to pay the bill. The police caught up with them on the Riviera where the two impostors, now without their make-up, were spending heavily.

Frauds like these have cost trusting philatelists a great deal of money. However, much more dangerous than an 'honest' forgery of an old classic are those colourful miniature prints that are nowadays advertised in newspapers and magazines. They all look like attractive stamps sets issued to commemorate, say, the late President Kennedy, to promote the Olympic Games and various other worthy causes, or to honour famous musicians, writers or artists, but in reality they are nothing but worthless junk designed to make enormous profits for unscrupulous businessmen.

Then there are the so-called bogus stamps. These are issued by countries that are either fictitious or merely small islands held legally, or even illegally, by entrepreneurs capitalizing on human folly. Among bogus stamps can also be ranked some unauthorized locals and issues of exiled governments residing in other stamp-issuing countries. There have been so many bogus issues that they perhaps deserve to be listed here: Abd-al Kuri, Alderney, Arab League, Bardsey Isl., Caldey Isl., Calf-of-Man, Carn Jar, Canna, Chan States, Commonwealth of Dalziel, Dahlak Isl., Davaar, Dhufar (province in Oman), Drake's Isl., Exiled Government of the Free City of Danzig, Eynhallow, Feripäga, Free Territory of Freedom, Gugh Isl., Herm, Hutt River Province, Ile Barbe, Isla de Bernera, Jethou, Karen State, Kugelmugel, Lihou, Lundy, Maluku Selatan, Marshall Islands, Nagaland, Ocussi-Ambeno, Order of the Knights of Malta, Pabay, Pidgeon Isl., Principality of Freiheit, Principality of Sealand, Principality of Thomond, Principality of Vikingland, Queen Maud Land, Redonda, Republic of Koneuwe, Republic of Lukonia, Republic of Morac, Romanian Government-in-Exile, Sanda, St. Kilda, Sark, Sedang, Shuna, Soay, Staffa, State of Oman, Stroma, Summer Islands, Tibet (exiled government), Toga, Walkoa Isl. The list does not include any of the sheikdoms whose issues do not meet many basic requirements stipulated by the UPU and FIP, so that their colourful labels are something resembling genuine stamps in appearance only.

Let us consider now a case that involved an authentic issue of one of the most renowned postal authorities of the world. The biggest forgery of all time had been defrauding the authorities for a number of years, took place in Great Britain, the home country of the postage stamp. In 1870 the British Post Office took over the administration of telegraph services operated hitherto by private firms. The rate for a twenty word wire was a shilling and the payment was acknowledged by a shilling stamp affixed on the back of the wire form. When the wire was dispatched the post kept the form on file for several years for possible claims. After a time the old wire forms were sold as scrap to paper mills for recycling. Auditing was limited to a comparison of dispatched wires and stamp sales receipts.

Then in 1898 a postal clerk broke the regulations and some old wire forms reached the hands of a stamp dealer. The dealer was naturally interested only in the stamps and thus he carefully washed them off the forms and started selling them. Collectors showed a great interest in the old shilling stamps that suddenly appeared on the market. And as true philatelists, they started studying and comparing in-the old shilling stamps that suddenly appeared on the market. And as true philatelists, they started studying and comparing individual specimens, trying to discover flaws and errors. They discovered that the stamps lacked watermarks. An investigation revealed that all the suspicious specimens were postal forgeries and that they had all come from the postal counter at the London Stock Exchange where one shilling stamps used to be sold in large quantities every day because the rate had covered most wires dispatched by the Exchange brokers.

The inquiry also showed that no broker had ever bothered to inspect the stamps against the light, much less compare them with shilling stamps bought elsewhere. Brokers testified that they had gladly left the job of affixing the stamps on the forms for the helpful clerk at the counter to do. It was then a matter of digging through the postal records to identify and find the clerk, who had since retired. The investigation revealed that over the years he had managed to defraud the post of £ 15,000, which was a lot of money in the 1870s. The post office, however, was unable tu sue its former employee because there was no evidence that it had been he who had forged the stamp in question. For philatelists, however, the whole affair represented a collector's dream. Whereas forgeries made to defraud collectors are totally worthless as philatelic material, those actually handled postally are extremely popular among collectors because they represent rarities of a kind.

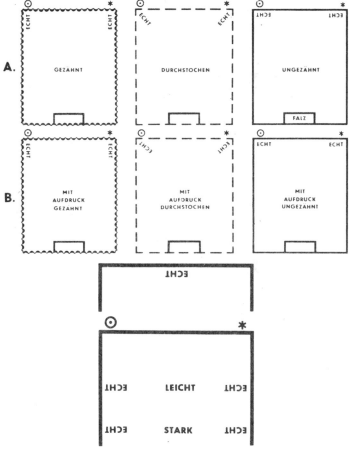

Location of experts' stamps and their meaning

Indeed, there have been many affairs involving forgeries that have caused great excitement in the world of philately. Following the Second World War the most widely publicized forgeries were those of the INSELPOST surcharges of German field post issues or forged HELA U-BOOT stamps, an issue that had never been actually used but received a lot of publicity after the war. Whenever forgeries are discovered, police and the philatelic press warn collectors both at home and abroad.

What can you do then to detect a forgery?

First of all, a true philatelist must study. He should know as much as possible about the issues of the country or period that he collects. He must know the circumstances under which his stamps originated, what printing processes were used for their manufacture, what errors, colour flaws and paper quality to expect. He should check the watermark and perforation. If he finds a hitherto unknown variety or an error he may even be lucky enough to have discovered a phenomenon that has not yet been catalogued. However, whenever you are in doubt, seek an expert's opinion. In every country there are a number of experts whose names appear in the philatelic press or can be obtained from philatelic clubs. Of course, even an expert may be wrong. However, official regulations stipulate the degree of his responsibility and the financial guarantee of his judgement.

Lower-value stamps should be taken to more experienced members of your club, while stamps of higher denominations or prices can be certified by the expert's handstamp. This is a small mark bearing the expert's name and it is placed on the back of the stamp according to fixed rules that every philatelist should become familiar with. For especially valuable stamps the expert will make out a certificate including photographic documentation. For a novice collector, however, the guarantee of a reputable philatelic dealer will suffice. Bona fide dealers naturally try to avoid forgeries and they guarantee their merchandise. In the past some dealers marked sold postage stamps with their own rubber stamps that were the equivalent of those of philatelic experts. Some stamps can bear approval stamps of two different experts, although this would apply to very rare stamps only. Whenever an expert comes across a forgery he is obliged to mark it as such to prevent unethical deals, possible claims and even lawsuits. There have been even cases when a stamp pronounced genuine by one expert was judged a forgery by another; such cases must be resolved by the court.

It is beyond the scope of this book to discuss in detail all the methods used by stamp experts to ascertain if a stamp is genuine. Sometimes a thorough inspection under a magnifying glass will do, sometimes the specimen must be projected on a screen under a much greater magnification, sometimes the expert may inspect the stamp under a special lamp emitting ultraviolet rays. In fact, these quartz lamps as they are termed can be bought at many philatelic stockists. However, before attempting any such examination, you should be familiar with the chemical composition of the inks used for the printing of your stamp and know what to expect.

Large catalogues register the existence of a great number of forged specimens in circulation by a small mark warning the collector against a perfunctory inspections and a rash acquisition of the stamp for a collection.

FAMOUS COLLECTORS

Their names are household words in the philatelic world and entire specialized books as well as numerous articles and studies have been written about them. Even auction catalogues often note that a certain stamp which is on sale came originally from a stamp magnate's collection. And for many a collector, to own such a stamp is equal to being knighted as a philatelist. The four most outstanding stamp collectors are: Ferrari, Burrus, Hind and Lichtenstein.

Prior to the First World War, Philippe la Renotière von Ferrari was the only man in the world who could rightfully claim to possess all stamps issued up to his time. Since then, nobody else has been able to make this statement.

Stamps were Ferrari's passion, to which he devoted his whole life. He did not have to worry about money because he had inherited a fortune from his mother and since he had no children to take care of he did nothing else but travel all over the world buying stamps that he thought were missing from his collection. The more popular or famous the stamp (especially if thought to exist only as a single specimen), the more he wanted to have it. The most expensive stamp in the world, the famous British Guiana, a few Mauritian issues, several missionary stamps, the famous Swedish printing error of the Three Shilling Banco, the only sheet of the Saxonian Three in existence, as well as thousands of other rarities were among his possessions. It is true that in his time the prices of rare stamps were not yet so prohibitive and stamps were still a hobby rather than an investment to be kept in a safe.

Ferrari in his quest for more and more stamps was willing to pay such good prices that his buyers and dealers saw in his obsession with stamps a perfect opportunity to get rich at his expense and thus the so-called 'Ferrarities', surreptitiously manufactured curios and specialities, came into being. Ferrari loved stamps more than anything else in the world but he never realized that to understand stamps means to study seriously these fascinating and colourful pieces of paper and that the more philatelic territories or periods one decides to make one's field interest the more one should know, the more one must study. And while Ferrari was interested in stamps of the whole world, he did not study much. His collection, apart from many genuine rarities, also contained a lot of philatelically worthless junk.

The eccentric baron was an Austrian subject but for most of his life he resided in Paris. Yet he was a great admirer of Imperial Germany and although France, his adopted home, ultimately found herself at war with Germany, he bequeathed his unique collection to the Imperial Postal Museum in Berlin, the first of its kind in the world, and at the time also the best. Ferrari did not live to see the end of the war. Shortly before his death in 1917, he sought refuge in neutral Switzerland and took with him also a part of his huge collection. His wishes, however, were never carried out because after the war the greater part of his treasury was confiscated as German property by the French, who decided to sell it and retain the receipts in lieu of German reparation payments.

But to sell the largest stamp collection of the world in an auction was not easy. First it was necessary to weed out all 'Ferrarities', fakes and forgeries. Only then could sets be put together that had a chance of being sold at an auction. Catalogues were printed and distributed a year in advance to give a chance to all prospective buyers from Europe and overseas to prepare themselves and attend. The majority of auction sales took place in Paris but some of the Ferrari stamps were also sold off abroad. Each auction was attended by buyers from all over the world and even those who were not collectors came to buy a set because it was fashionable to do so. Philatelists arrived in Paris because they saw a chance to obtain something that was usually very difficult to come by on the regular market. Millionaires, especially those from overseas whose money could buy them practically anything in impoverished post-war Europe, as well as sovereigns who also collected stamps naturally realized very clearly that any interest shown on their part would immediately drive the price of the stamp in question sky high and therefore they sent agents to bid on their behalf. The auctions also offered a huge quantity of less expensive stamps that could be successfully bid for by normal collectors. In the end, ex-Ferrari stamps found their way into untold thousands of collections all over the world and never again will there be anybody who could claim to own all stamps of the world. Besides, modern philately is something totally different from what ended as an obsession of baron Philippe la Renotière von Ferrari.

Maurice Burrus had no aristocratic ancestors but his wealth equalled that of any medieval king. He made a huge fortune in tobacco, and on his retirement moved to Switzerland. There he devoted all his time to his one and only hobby, philately. Being a businessman and perhaps having learned a lesson from Ferrari's case, he realized that there was no sense in globe-trotting in a futile attempt to acquire philatelic rarities. In fact, in his time practically all rarities had been discovered and identified, so that collectors with enough financial means at their disposal had only to wait for an auction. It is also possible that Burrus knew his stamps and was hard to fool. According to philatelic lore, Burrus, although a multimillionaire, never bought a stamp without a thorough deliberation.

In April 1922, the Hôtel Drouot auction house of Paris put the rarest of all Ferrari's stamps on the market; it was a damaged, unattractive 1856 British Guiana. Most of the world's famous philatelists as well as buyers for several sovereigns attended the auction The auctioneer stated that every prospective buyer had had a chance to inspect the stamp (which in itself was a most unusual thing) and that no further claims would be allowed. Immediately upon the start of the bidding the price skyrocketed up to 200,000 francs. Then the bidding was confined to two persons only, an English dealer named Griebert and Maurice Burrus. In the end, Griebert acquired the stamp for 300,000 francs.

However, soon after the auction had closed, Burrus claimed that the famous Guiana was a forgery. It remains a mystery why he bid as high as 290,000 francs if he was so sure that the stamp was a worthless piece of paper. It seems more likely that he knew it was genuine but was sorry to see the unique stamp go to another collector. The new owner exhibited the stamp at several major philatelic exhibitions on various continents; the stamp was viewed by hundreds of thousands of philatelists as well as by many experts, and nobody found anything that would justify Burrus' claim. Perhaps the stamp was slightly too expensive even for a tobacco king.

After Burrus' death his collections were auctioned and remain in circulation under the honourable designation *ex-Burrus*. At these auctions not only the rarest specimens were sold but also cheaper stamps that even average collectors could afford. Several such auctions were held in 1962—1964 by Robson Lowe's of Britain. In 1964, H.R. Harmer's sold the most valuable of the ex-Burrus stamps, the Missionary Hawaii Two Cent, for more than two million pounds.

Arthur Hind, U.S. financier and industrialist, appeared on the philatelic scene for the first time in 1922 at the Hôtel Drouot in Paris. It was he who bought the British Guiana One Cent because Griebert merely acted as his agent. The most expensive stamp of the world was taken overseas. However, Hind was never regarded as much of a philatelist although it is hard to say whether he bought stamps only as an investment or whether they were his true hobby. Hind's name is also associated with a philatelic legend.

The legend concerns a poor orphaned boy from one of the Southern states of the U.S.A. When he reached the minimum age requirement, he enlisted as a sailor's apprentice and sailed away with his ship. On his departure, his best friend gave him an envelope with all kinds of old stamps as a parting gift. As a sailor the young man had no time to spend on stamps and he opened the envelope only years later when he discovered it among his personal effects. To his astonishment, one of the stamps in the packet turned out to be a stamp which he had seen many times in the world press. It was an 1856 British Guiana Red and only one specimen was known to exist. And since the young man had a sharp mind, he realized that the best person to whom he could sell the stamp was the owner of the other specimen, i.e. Arthur Hind. The two are purported to have met secretly and alone. The legend goes that Hind bought the stamp from the young sailor and immediately burned it in the flame of a candle, although the boy's specimen was in a much better condition than his own. Hind simply could not risk the public learning that his specimen, photographed so many times as unique, was not in fact the only one of its kind in existence.

Hind died in 1933 and his extensive collection was also auctioned in several parts. However, the famous British Guinea was found to be missing. Hind's wife stated that her husband had given the stamp away as a gift but she did not know to whom. The unique stamp was found only much later; it had been deposited in a sealed envelope in one of Hind's bank vaults. At the auction, however, bidders did not go even as high as the reserve price and the stamp had to be taken off the block only to be sold later in a private deal. It was publicly displayed again only as late as 1970 and was sold to a consortium of American businessmen for U.S. $ 280,000.

A. F. Lichtenstein, another American millionaire, was an ardent philatelist and he put tohether several outstanding collections that he exhibited at various stamp exhibitions. Thanks to his wealth he was able to acquire a number of famous rarities, among other things also several Mauritian issues, and owned the world's most expensive entire, a letter bearing two Mauritian Reds. His daughter, Louise Boyd Dale, inherited her love for postage stamps from her father who gave her the letter as a gift. The two travelled together a lot and appeared several times at various European exhibitions. According to pre-war catalogues, their exhibits on display at a European exhibition (and which represented only a minor part of the entire collection) were insured for one hundred thousand pounds. Both Lichtenstein and his daughter frequently lectured and wrote on stamps and philately and Mrs. Dale was even elected a honorary member of many leading philatelic associations and clubs, among them the prestigious Royal Philatelic Society in London.

The Lichtenstein-Dale collections were sold at auctions in 1968. The letter with the two Mauritian Reds was sold by H.R. Harmer's of New York for U.S. $ 380,000. The auction was broadcast live both on radio and TV but it was more of a sensation than a truly philatelic affair. What the broadcast somewhat failed to emphasize was that both Mrs. Dale and her father knew a lot about stamps and did much for the advancement of philately.

All in all, there have been many philatelists who put together famous stamp collections. And they were not always multimillionaires who could afford to raise their bids by tens of thousands of dollars at a time. Many postal museums have ordinary stamp enthusiasts to thank for their enormous riches. For all those who collected stamps not to invest money but because they loved them, the name of Thomas Keay Tapling deserves to be mentioned here. During his life, T. K. Tapling gathered a collection whose collector's value is practically impossible to estimate in terms of money. The Tapling Collection documents so many issues that it has in fact become a living textbook of philately. At the end of his life T. K. Tapling did not take the collection to a dealer to sell but gave it to the British Museum where it can be admired by the public.

THE ARRANGEMENT OF A COLLECTION

Finally you have reached that happy moment when you are able to start assembling your own collection. You should clear the table, wash your hands and empty the contents of all those envelopes, folders and boxes in which you have been saving your stamps. Let us concern ourselves with stamps first, leaving postal stationery and entires aside for a moment.

Where have you obtained your material? Well, from old correspondence of all kinds, from your friends and acquaintances. Your material does not have to be from the classic philatelic period. Sometimes even stamps only a few years old can be very interesting and can have a great philatelic potential. For example, just try to compare the individual colour varieties produced by the printing house in subsequent runs of the same stamp.

The best method is to start by collecting your own country's stamps and go progressively back into its history. A cut-off point is also advisable, be it the end of the Second World War, the turn of the century, etc. If you decide to build your collection round a specific topic, such as roses, horse breeding, sports, etc., you can also start by buying those familiar cellophane packets showing stamps with your favourite topic that are displayed in the windows of philatelic dealers and agencies. These packets contain stamps from all over the world and can often be bought even in souvenir and novelty shops.

After some time you will undoubtedly have acquired a number of doublets that you will want to exchange for other stamps you may need for your collection. Attend the meeting of your local philatelic club and start swapping your stamps with other fellow members. Do not attend large official auctions in the beginning. Many clubs hold small auctions of their own where members' doublets are sold: this is where you should start buying stamps, naturally only after thoroughly inspecting the stamps offered for sale. Since each item on sale is numbered, it is enough to take down the number and to decide how much you would be willing to pay for the item. The rules usually call for an immediate payment so don't count on being able to pop home to get the money! The auctioneer will always call the number of the item and the price requested and bidding will then take place. The speed of the bidding will take some time to get used to, but after you have had some practice you will be surprised to learn that even at small auctions one is occasionally able to pick up good buys; stamps, entires and covers are sometimes sold well under the price listed in official catalogues.

Prices of Stamps and Other Philatelic Material

There exists a number of catalogues that you can, and sometimes must, consult. The most frequently used catalogues in Europe are the German *Michel's*, the Swiss *Zumstein's* and the French *Yvert's*, which list the official price in Deutschemarks, Swiss francs and French francs respectively. Actually, the prices listed are publisher's prices that are an excellent basis for exchange because they show comparative values. Stamps are usually bought and sold at lower prices. The situation led to great confusion and catalogue publishers who are members of the ASCAT have decided to list prices in national currencies. Some catalogues are updated annually, other specialized

Symbols used in philatelic catalogues

catalogues appear only once in several years. However, many philatelists use older editions, so always make sure about the conversion or adjustment rates before using a catalogue as a basis for bargaining. Besides the large catalogues listed above there are also a number of smaller ones published by various dealers and agencies. The best-known German publication of this kind is *Borek's*. The prices listed there depend largely on the stock that the dealership has but since *Borek's* is a large philatelic emporium many philatelists go by its catalogue; the numbering is identical to that used by *Michel's*.

The three major European catalogues that have been mentioned here deal primarily with European issues but *Yvert's* has also a very good comprehensive section on overseas issues and is therefore often used as a reference for deals involving overseas stamps, too. On the other hand, it would be foolish to use anything but the *Michel Special* for deals involving the issues of Germany, including the old German states, German-occupied territories, colonies and posts in Africa and Asia. *Zumstein's* is the best catalogue for Swiss and Liechtenstein issues. All these catalogues also provide information on all kinds of varieties.

As well as stamp catalogues there are also postal stationery ones. There are no catalogues for entires, though, but stamp catalogues sometimes list the prices of stamps on entires.

Stamps are listed in catalogues by the date of issue. The number and description of the issue is followed by two price columns; the first, headed by an asterisk, shows prices of unused stamps, the other, which is headed by a circle with a dot in the centre, designates postally used, i.e. cancelled, stamps. Sometimes a third column with two asterisks precedes the unused stamps column; the price listed there applies to stamps in mint condition, i.e. those that have the gum intact and have been never mounted in a collection. The mint stamp price reflects a kind of vogue discussed earlier in this book. Dealers try to capitalize on the trend and sell their stock at the highest prices possible and, unfortunately, there are some collectors who have adopted this somewhat artificial concept of stamp evaluation. Sometimes there is also a fourth column denoted by a rectangle with diagonals, i.e. a stylized letter. Prices listed there apply to stamps found on entires. Other symbols designating other categories will be found in the introductory section of every catalogue.

Beginners can often make do with smaller national catalogues that do not list any printing errors or varieties or other than original usages. Large world catalogues are usually available in club libraries.

Most auction catalogues evaluate their stock on the basis of large European catalogues, sometimes also major overseas ones like the American *Scott's*. The second column in auction catalogues lists reserved prices at which the bidding will start. Even if you do not attend an auction you can find a lot of interesting facts in its catalogue. Auction catalogues are often richly illustrated and apart from this, just browsing through the text will give you a comprehensive picture of what can be found on the market and at what price. Even a catalogue that is several years old can be a great textbook of philately, that is perhaps equalled only by a visit to a major stamp exhibition.

Preparation of Stamps

You have now spread your stamps in front of you on a desk. The stamps have come from various sources and are in all kinds of conditions: some are used, some unused, others quite soiled, and some with remnants of old hinges on the back because they have passed through many collections. Your first task will be to sort your stamps in two groups. The first will contain those that can be used as they are. These will be the unused specimens and cancelled stamps that have already been washed, dried and pressed. In the other group place those that require such treatment, especially specimens that have been cut out from a cover, or used undamaged stamps with remnants of the original gum. Take a basin or a bowl filled with lukewarm water and immerse the stamps with the backing in it. It is quite useless to wash stamps that have been already treated because any subsequent washing will affect the colour and general condition of the stamp. Hot water should be also avoided because it may discolour your stamps.

After a short immersion the gum will become partially dissolved and the stamp can be easily slid off the backing. Never use force to remove the stamp from the paper! Leave the stamp in the water for a little longer to make sure that all gum washes off properly. Check lightly with your fingertip whether the back is still slippery. If it is not, the stamp is ready for drying. This is best done with the stamp placed between two or more strong blotters inserted in a thick book. Be sure that your stamps do not touch each other and that no corner is bent; a bent corner can break when the stamp is pressed. It is advisable to place a heavy object on the book or even to use a small press for a day. Improperly dried stamps would stick to mint specimens that have the gum still intact. These would require another washing that would dissolve the gum and devalue the stamps.

Inspection and Classification of Philatelic Material

You can now spread your washed and mint stamps on the desk again and remove all damaged ones, e.g. classics cut into the design (centre), stamps missing a perforation tooth or a corner and, of course, all torn specimens regardless of the fact that the tear may not be visible on the face, as well as all thinned specimens that have been forcefully removed from the cover. The remaining material is to be divided in two groups. In the first place those stamps that you intend to mount in your collection; the rest will be used to exchange for other stamps. Stamps that you intend to swap should be placed in a stock-book and arranged by countries or topics. Material for your collection should be carefully inspected stamp by stamp under a magnifying lens. This is not done to find any defects because damaged stamps should already have been rejected but because the magnification will sometimes reveal differences in the design that are impossible to see with the naked eye. Possible varieties are listed in collectors' catalogues, or they may be pointed out to you by more experienced fellow collectors.

Each stamp should be then inspected for a watermark, if the issue has any, because the watermark can sometimes make identification easier. For instance, German stamps with the Hindenburg medallion have watermarks either in the form of a rhomboid grille or a swastika, depending on the issue. Watermarked stamps are best inspected either against light, or with the reverse up and slightly tilted towards a lamp. A watermark can also be positively found if the stamp is placed face down in a small black dish sold by most philatelic stockists. The back is then wetted with a drop of spirit of alcohol or benzine. These agents are safe even on mint stamps because they do not dissolve the gum. Wetted stamps must be thoroughly dried afterwards and all the spirit must be allowed to evaporate. It is also advisable to note down the watermark because frequent wetting will affect the colours.

As a thorough student of stamps you should never forget to check the perforation because you might be able to discover one not listed in catalogues. The stamp is placed against a perforation gauge available at any philatelic dealer

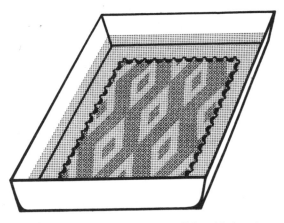

Checking paper watermarks in a dish with benzine

and the stamp perforation is compared with the gauges provided until the black dots of a particular gauge fall centrally in with the perforation of the stamp. Some countries use different sized pin bars for vertical and horizontal perforations and in such a case you must check two adjacent sides of your stamp. Again, do not forget to note down the perforation on a piece of paper and keep it with the stamps for further reference, so you won't have to re-gauge your entire collection. During inspection and classification each stamp has to be lifted and handled many times, and to pick up a stamp from the desk with one's fingers without crumpling the little piece of paper is not easy. Tweezers should therefore always be used. At first you will think that the tweezers are clumsy and that it would be better to use your fingers. All it really takes is a bit of practice. Soon you will get used to it and won't go anywhere without a pair. A good pair of tweezers must be springy and must have no pointed or sharp-edged tips. Philatelic stockists always carry several types to choose from.

Albums

Children's albums have a page for every country and each page is divided into a number of frames. To make the albums more attractive, some frames have black-and-white illustrations of foreign stamps. It is quite immaterial in what order the child mounts the stamps in an album; it is sufficient if he or she is able to sort stamps by countries.

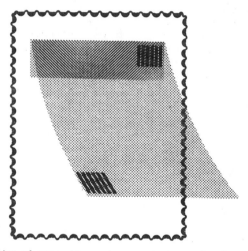

Use of paper hinges to mount stamps in albums

General adult collectors usually use albums with card paper sheets of various kinds and of the size used for exhibitions. Each sheet is loose and sets of such sheets can be bound with screws or springs into binders. These albums may also have preprinted frames for individual stamps and frequently feature black-and-white reproductions of basic stamps of each individual set. Although the frames are arranged symmetrically along the vertical axis so that the sheets appear attractive and orderly, albums of this kind hinder philatelic creativity because they do not give the collector a chance to mount any varieties for which there are no frames provided. For example, if a collector discovers two colour varieties of a stamp he must mount only one because there is no space for the other on the album sheet. In no case do such albums provide space for differences in watermarks, perforations, paper quality, inks, etc. In addition, preprinted albums do not allow for mounting cut-squares with interesting special postmarks, much less postal stationery or entires.

Individually conceived collections use fine screen-printed card paper. The screen is used to make sure that all exhibits are mounted symmetrically. Another possibility is to use purely white card paper on which the collector can mount his stamps in any arrangement or layout and draw thin black frames around each stamp. This layout is very attractive and very flexible since it permits the collector to include in his collection any type of material but it requires a lot of time, patience and also skill.

One of the perennial questions discussed by philatelists is how to mount unused stamps in albums. The classical method requires that unused stamps be attached to the sheet in the same way as used specimens, letters, cut-squares, and wrappers, i.e. by using a white adhesive paper tape hinge.

However, advertisements in philatelic magazines often promote black or white mounts with a transparent film top, or the film alone to be used to protect stamps in albums. Although the elastic film will protect both the face and the gummed back, the method has its disadvantages. First of all, used and unused stamps are treated differently which lowers the aesthetic appeal of the collection. The price is also higher than that of hinges, which is an important factor in large collections. Last but not least, despite the considerable labour required to etch the film chemical to make it adhere to the paper, the film does not stop the stamps from becoming dislodged and falling out when the sheet is handled. Please note that even exhibits displayed at large international collections feature priceless rare classics mounted on simple hinges.

Stamps can be greatly damaged by corner mounts used for photographs. Some collectors use these mounts occasionally to display entires, miniature or printing sheets and postal stationery. The mounts are made of cellophane which will oxidize in time and the paper will turn brown in those places that touch the mounts. But even if the mounts are made of a chemically stable material, there is still a danger that the sharp edge of the mount will cut the inserted paper if it is taken out for inspection too often. Again, the best method is to use the classical gummed paper hinges or transparent covers.

A few words should be added about the graphic layout of a collection. Decorative drawings on title pages that are intended to convey the theme of the collection are best left to enthuasiastic young collectors who express their joy at creativity in this way. A serious collector should limit himself to simple and purely graphic means, preferably a well-chosen and well-executed script. There are collectors who have material of

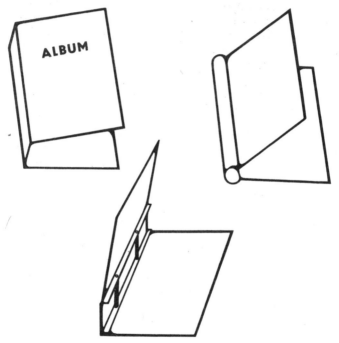

Spring and screw-held binders for album sheets

undisputed philatelic value and yet they mistake their album for a scrapbook. It is of course praiseworthy that such collectors view their collections as documents of a particular period but to display, say, newspaper clippings dealing with the Lakehurst disaster among Zeppelin letters is a philatelic step backward. If the maker of the collection wants to mention the event at all, he should document it on philatelic material, e.g. a wreck letter, or he should limit himself to a single line caption.

It is also bad to document an exhibition with photographs if stamps or postal stationery have been issued for the occasion. If the author feels that such material is not enough to emphasize the importance of the event, he can use various postmarks, cachets, and entires conveyed by special carriers like balloons, mailcoaches, etc. On the other hand a reproduction (facsimile) of a departmental decree on the introduction of a new type of stamp, the establishment of new post offices in newly annexed territories and other such documents do represent material of a definite philatelic interest. Naturally, all such auxiliary exhibits must be relevant to the stamps or postmark exhibited; they must be the *raison d'être* for what the collector intends to document in his collection.

Topicalists also frequently try to enrich their collections with material that has no place there, e.g. pictures of astronauts or newspaper features on satellite launchings in collections devoted to space flights, etc. Remember that all these things can be, and indeed must be, documented on philatelic material. Thanks to the immense popularity of the topic, special issues appear in the launching country and elsewhere to hail each new mission and some postal authorities will commemorate space flights with new issues, hold philatelic exhibitions and bring out a host of postmarks, entires, etc., so that collectors cannot complain of lack of available material. The same applies essentially to various other topics, be it sports, the Olympic Games, flowers, wild animals, art reproductions or, say, the development of writing and book printing. The basic rule which should always be kept in mind is that you are building a philatelic collection in which non-philatelic material has no place whatsoever. Remember that all exhibition juries give penalty points for use of non-philatelic material in exhibits; this lowers the merit of an otherwise valuable collection, which its creator might have spent many nights assembling.

A very important feature of any collection are the captions. It would be erroneous to believe that you should include everything you know about your stamps in the captions. On the contrary, one or two word captions are considered the best.

Anything you know about your stamps, postal stationery or entires should be documented philatelically rather than verbally. Printing errors, paper varieties or printing processes employed in the manufacture of your stamps should be documented by separate specimens. If the specimen illustrates a minor flaw indiscernible at first sight, it is best to draw a small black arrow on the album page, pointing at the feature in question, or to cut an arrow from black paper and fix it on the page in such a way as to have it overlap the stamp and end at the flaw (e.g. an over-inked letter, a blotch, etc.). There are collections (and exhibition juries judge them to be of considerable philatelic interest and evaluate them accordingly with prizes) that analyse certain issues in such detail that several album sheets may be devoted to a single stamp, each specimen documenting a particular error, flaw or variety, all discovered by the creator of the collection. Such collections are called study collections and besides errors and flaws they also document unusual employment of the stamp, e.g. a postage stamp used as a postage due, delivery or other type of stamp, but without a surcharge because the latter changes the function of a stamp in an authorized way. A philatelic curiosity would be, for example, a stamp that had been originally issued as postage, then surcharged to make a postage due and subsequently used to frank a letter.

Let us return to captions and scripts, however. Caligraphy, naturally without excessive flourishes and scrolls, is of course best but it is not easy for an unskilled hand to do, especially since the script is to be consistent throughout the entire collection. Besides, no collection is ever finished because you may always discover something to add and if you cannot be sure of having the same script throughout, it is better to adopt a less demanding method. Letterpress texts naturally look very attractive but require a lot of time and are quite expensive. The most universally available methods are therefore typewritten captions and accompanying texts. Again, there are two possibilities. The more attractive one is to type directly on to the album sheet but one must make sure to use a ribbon that will produce letters of uniform blackness throughout the collection without making them blurred, and besides, most typewriters for home use do not feature wide carriages that would hold the album sheet. It is therefore better to type your captions on strips of paper of a similar colour to that of the mounting sheet and to paste them on to the latter. Another advantage is that the strips can be replaced relatively easily several times, which will allow you to mount captions with foreign language texts if your collection is exhibited abroad.

In conclusion, let us make a few remarks. Never underestimate the aesthetic aspect of your collection. Exhibition juries always consider the aesthetic value of every collection and an unattractive layout will lower your score. In any case, a nicely arranged collection will always be a greater inspiration to continue working on it than a stock-book crammed with the same stamps. All your guests to whom you proudly show your work will enjoy clean, neat, attractively arranged album sheets. On the other hand, the graphic aspects of a collection cannot be overestimated, either, because after all, the primary concern of every collection must be the philatelic material, its rarity, completeness and detailed study. Even a most beautifully arranged collection will be judged poor if it consists of scanty and poorly documented material. Remember that no arrangement in the world can compensate for a lack of philatelic merit in a collection.

MAJOR PHILATELIC ORGANIZATIONS

Your source of inspiration, your closest helpers and mentors will always be found in your philatelic club. Be sure to select one that is not only close to your home but whose particular specialization, programme, meeting schedules and general atmosphere suit you best. You need not be much concerned about the county (district, regional) and national organizations unless you become a club official. All philatelic clubs in a country are either directly or indirectly represented in the national philatelic association. Only these national associations may become members of the International Philatelic Federation or FIP *(Fédération internationale de philatélie)*. Only one philatelic association from each country can represent that country's philatelists on this international philatelic forum. At present, more than 50 national associations are members of FIP.

The Federation was founded in Paris in 1929 and, according to its 1972 statute, its aim is to promote philately internationally, to strive for friendly relations and cooperation among philatelists for the preservation of peace and friendship among nations; to support national as well as international undertakings promoting philately; to protect the interests of philatelists; and to prevent racial, religious and political discrimination among member associations.

The highest body of FIP is the Congress, which meets annually. The Congress is attended by representatives of member associations. Resolutions must be passed by a majority of votes. In the interim period all affairs of the Federation are conducted by the Executive Committee composed of the President of FIP and four Executive Committee members. All are elected for four years. Philatelists are mostly interested in the work of the individual specialized FIP commissions whose concerns are: classic collections, topical collections, youth, entires, aerophilatelics, pre-stamp era documents and philatelic literature.

Apart from these major commissions there are also commissions specializing in philatelic press and propaganda, protection against undesirable issues, preservation of outstanding collections, postal history and anti-forgery activities. Besides proposing measures concerning their special interests, the commissions also propose changes in exhibition rules. Adopted rules become a model for those of all exhibitions organized by FIP member associations. Every year several major international exhibitions are held under the auspices of FIP, one being usually designated officially a World Exhibition if its concept meets the prerequisites for such an honourable title.

Another world-wide philatelic organization is the International Federation of Aerophilatelic Associations known as FISA *(Fédération internationale de societés aérophilatéliques)*. FISA was founded in 1960 and like FIP, it unites national aerophilatelic organizations rather than clubs or individuals. FISA co-ordinates its activities with those of FIP and it is possible that the two will merge in the future. FISA as a specialized organization has done much to promote aerophilately and as it is concerned with the specific problems of this branch of philately, it has a great influence on the concepts and arrangements of airmail collections. FISA also holds annual congresses that elect its President and a Board of Directors who remain in office for two years. Exhibitions are held under the auspices of the Federation and among other things feature balloon races.

Mention should also be made of the International Association of Philatelic Journalists and Authors known as AIJP *(Association internationale des journalistes philatéliques)* which unites professional writers on philately. The Association holds annual congresses where the members discuss organizational matters and exchange news and experience. The President and a six-member Board are elected for three years. The membership is personal, i.e. the members do not represent any national philatelic or other organization.

A smaller but nevertheless prestigious international body is the International Association of Philatelic Experts known as AIEP *(Association internationale des experts philatéliques)*, uniting leading philatelic experts recommended for membership by national philatelic associations. AIEP also convenes annually to discuss such important problems as anti-forgery activities, co-ordination of expertise as well as interests of the members. The membership is also individual and in order to be accepted each candidate must meet high professional standards.

PLACE-NAME INDEX   *Numbers in italics indicate illustrations*